MATH GIRLS

TALK ABOUT

INTEGERS

Fundamental Skills for Advanced Mathematics

BY HIROSHI YUKI

Author of MATH GIRLS

TRANSLATED BY TONY GONZALEZ

MATH GIRLS TALK ABOUT THE INTEGERS

Originally published as *Sūgaku Gāru No Himitsu Nōto Seisū De Asobō*
Copyright © 2013 Hiroshi Yuki
Softbank Creative Corp., Tokyo

English translation © 2014 by Tony Gonzalez
Edited by Joseph Reeder and M.D. Hendon
Cover design by Kasia Bytnerowicz

Published 2014 by

Bento Books, Inc.
Austin, Texas 78732

bentobooks.com

ISBN 978-1-939326-24-9 (hardcover)
ISBN 978-1-939326-23-2 (trade paperback)
Library of Congress Control Number: 2014945466

Printed in the United States of America
First edition, September 2014

Math Girls Talk About
The Integers

To My Readers

This book is a collection of conversations between Miruka, Tetra, Yuri, and our narrator.

If there are places where you don't understand what they're talking about, or equations you don't understand, feel free to skip over those parts. But please do your best to keep up with them.

That's the best way to make yourself part of the conversation.

—Hiroshi Yuki

Cast of Characters

I am your narrator. I'm a junior in high school, and I love math. Equations in particular.

Miruka is my age. She's so good at math, it's scary. She has long black hair and wears metal frame glasses.

Tetra is one year younger than me, and a bundle of energy. She cuts her hair short and has big, beautiful eyes.

Yuri is my cousin, an eighth grader. She has a chestnut ponytail and excels at logic.

Ms. Mizutani is our school librarian.

Mom is, well, just my mom.

Contents

Prologue

Our days are marked by repetition: Morning, noon, night. Morning, noon, night. Our years are marked by repetition: Spring, summer, autumn, winter. Spring, summer, autumn, winter. We mark the passing of our lives with repetition: yesterday, today, tomorrow.

Repetition gives rise to groups. Groups give rise to numbers. Repetition has rhythm, and from rhythm arises music. We live our lives dancing to repetition: 1–2–3, 1–2–3.

We discover rules in our dance. Rules for moving forward. Rules for leaping ahead. Rules that determine the next step.

We discover patterns in our dance. Patterns in the hands of clocks. Patterns in cards. Patterns in random doodles.

Come with us to search for the rhythms in repetition, for the rules in patterns. We'll find magic in puzzles, and games in tests.

Come, and join the dance.

CHAPTER 1

Checking for Multiples

"You don't have to understand how
rules work to use them..."

1.1 MULTIPLES OF THREE

Yuri   "Hey, cuz! I have a quiz for you."

Me   "I love how you keep thinking you're going to trip me up
        some day."

Yuri   "That day might be today. Tell me this: is 123,456,789
        a multiple of 3?"

Problem

Is 123,456,789 a multiple of 3?

My cousin Yuri was in eighth grade, and we'd
pretty much grown up together. She lived just up
the street, and often came over to read books and
work on math problems.

Me   "I guess you just made up a big number by stringing
          together the digits 1 through 9?"

Yuri   "That's beside the point. Is it a multiple of 3?"

Me   "Yes."

Yuri   "Couldn't you at least *pretend* you had to think hard to
          get the answer?"

Answer

Yes, 123,456,789 is a multiple of 3.

Me   "For such an easy question? No. All you have to do is
          add all the digits in the number and check if the sum is
          a multiple of 3."

Determining multiples of 3

To see if a number is a multiple of 3, add its digits and check if
the sum is a multiple of 3. For example, to check if 123,456,789
is a multiple of 3, add

$$1 + 2 + 3 + 4 + 5 + 6 + 7 + 8 + 9 = 45.$$

45 is a multiple of 3, so 123,456,789 must be too.

Yuri   "You cheated. Somehow."

Me   "How is applying a rule cheating?"

Yuri   "Well for one thing, how did you add up 1 through 9 so
          fast?"

Me   "I had it memorized."

Yuri   "You have *got* to be joking."

Me   "Well, actually I memorized that the sum of 1 through
            10 is 55, so I just subtracted 10 from that."

$$1 + 2 + 3 + 4 + 5 + 6 + 7 + 8 + 9 + 10 = 55$$

$$1 + 2 + 3 + 4 + 5 + 6 + 7 + 8 + 9 \qquad = 45$$

Yuri   "Forgive me if I don't waste precious brain cells remem-
            bering that."

Me   "You don't really need to. It's almost just as easy to sum
            it up using paired tens."

Yuri   "Meaning?"

Me   "You can add the first 1 and the last 9 to get 10, right?
            Then do the same with 2 and 8, 3 and 7, and 4 and 6.
            That gives you four 10s and a 5 left over. Add those up
            to get 45."

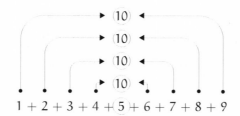

Paired tens make this addition problem easy

Yuri   "Now *that* I like!"

Me   "How'd you come up with the problem?"

Yuri   "My math teacher showed us how to check if a number
            is a multiple of 3 by adding its digits and seeing if the
            sum is a multiple of 3."

Me   "So it's cheating when I use a rule, but not when you
            do?"

Yuri   "Glad to see you're catching on."

1.2 ANOTHER CHECK

Me   "How about giving this one a shot?"

Problem

Is 103,690,369 a multiple of 3?

Yuri   "Piece of cake. Let's see, $1 + 0 + 3 + 6 + 9 + 0 + 3 + 6 + 9$ is...uh...37. And 37 isn't a multiple of 3, so 103,690,369 isn't either!"

Answer

103,690,369 is **not** a multiple of 3.

Me   "That's right. Took you long enough, though."

Yuri   "Well excuse me, Mr. Human Calculator."

Me   "Actually, you don't need to calculate anything for this one."

Yuri   "Not even paired tens?"

Me   "Nope. When you use the rule, you can ignore digits that are already multiples of three."

Yuri   "Whaaat?"

Me   "You only need to add up the digits that *aren't* multiples of three."

$$1 + \underbrace{0 + 3 + 6 + 9 + 0 + 3 + 6 + 9}_{\text{you can ignore these multiples of 3}}$$

Yuri   "That only leaves a 1!"

Me   "That's right. And since 1 isn't a multiple of 3, this number can't be a multiple of 3."

Yuri   "More cheating!"

Me   "Not at all. Do you see how adding a multiple of 3 to another multiple of 3 just gives you a new multiple of 3?"

Yuri   "I guess."

Me   "And how adding a multiple of 3 to a number that *isn't* a multiple of 3 *won't* result in a multiple of 3?"

Yuri   "Hmm..."

1.3 MATHEMATICAL PROOF

Me   "It sounds like you haven't convinced yourself that this rule works."

Yuri   "What do you mean?"

Me   "That you obviously know how to *use* the rule, but you don't understand it well enough to really get it."

Yuri   "Yeah, maybe."

Yuri frowns and twists her hair with a finger.

Me   "If you really want to be convinced, I can show you a mathematical proof."

Yuri   "What's a proof?"

Me   "It's where you apply certain conditions to show that some mathematical statement must logically be true."

Yuri   "Not seeing why I would want to do that."

Me   "Because it gets rid of maybes. It's a way of showing that you're absolutely, positively right."

Yuri	"I'm always absolutely, positively right, but maybe these proof things would be handy in convincing others."
Me	"I figured you'd see the attraction."
Yuri	"So show me how to do them."
Me	"Let's start by limiting the discussion to numbers less than 1000."

What we want to prove

Let n be an integer, with $0 \leqslant n < 1000$ (i.e., $n = 0, 1, 2, \ldots, 998, 999$), and let A_n be the sum of the digits in n.

  Then the following are true:

① If A_n is a multiple of 3, then n is a multiple of 3.

② If A_n is not a multiple of 3, then n is not a multiple of 3.

Yuri	"Well that was easy."
Me	"No, no—this isn't the proof. This is what we want to prove."
Yuri	"I don't remember wanting to prove anything about all these n's and A_n's and all."
Me	"We need those to precisely describe what we're doing. Trust me, if you just say things like 'this number' or 'that number,' everything ends up becoming much more confusing."
Yuri	"Why can't we just use an actual number, like 123?"
Me	"You can. In fact, a lot of times it's best to start out with a specific example like that."

Yuri	"Here goes, then. $1 + 2 + 3 = 6$, and 6 is a multiple of 3. To check if that really worked, you divide 123 by 3, and get . . . uh . . . 41. Since we got a whole number as the answer, that means 123 is a multiple of 3, too, so the rule worked. Done!"
Me	"Not done. All you did is verify that the proposition works for one specific number."
Yuri	"And that's wrong how?"
Me	"It isn't *wrong* at all. Like I always say, examples are the key to understanding. What you just did shows you know exactly what it is we want to prove."
Yuri	"But . . . ?"
Me	"But an example isn't a proof. We want to be more . . . general."
Yuri	"And what does that mean?"
Me	"Letting $n = 123$ is what's called a specific case, and you showed that this statement ① works for that particular value of n. But you can't do that for every number, 0 through 999."
Yuri	"You doubt my abilities, do you?"
Me	"Let me rephrase. Sure, you *could* check every number, but it would be an awful lot of work, right?"
Yuri	"Yeah, and I'm allergic to lots of work."
Me	"Then think of letter variables in math as a way to avoid all that."
Yuri	"Convince me."
Me	"It's called 'generalization through the introduction of a variable.' For example, we can rewrite this n using a, b, c, like this."

Representing numbers as letters

We can represent an integer n $(0 \leqslant n < 1000)$ using letters a, b, c as follows:
$$n = 100a + 10b + c$$

Here, each of a, b, c is one of $0, 1, 2, 3, 4, 5, 6, 7, 8, 9$.

Yuri   "You're making things worse."

Me   "It's not that bad. Can you rewrite $100a + 10b + c$ using multiplication symbols?"

Yuri   "Like this?"
$$100 \times a + 10 \times b + c$$

Me   "Right. See how we're adding 100 times a, 10 times b, and c?"

Yuri   "Yeah, but what's a?"

Me   "It's the digit in the hundreds place of the number. And b is the tens digit, and c is the ones digit."

Yuri crosses her arms and frowns.

1.4 DEFINING THINGS FOR YOURSELF

Me   "Something bothering you?"

Yuri   "Yeah. How can you know all that? That the hundreds digit is a and all."

Me   "It's not that I know what it is, I just defined things that way. Those are definitions I made to use in the proof I'm going to do."

Yuri   "You can just make stuff up like that?"

Me   "Sure, you can define things any way you like. I guess it seems weird at first, but when you use equations to work problems out, defining your own variables can be a real help. I named these variables a, b, c, but anything would do. Use whatever letters you like."

Yuri   "Go on then."

Me   "Okay, getting back to the problem. We rewrote n as

$$n = 100a + 10b + c.$$

We're using a to represent the number in the hundreds place, b as the number in the tens place, and c as the number in the ones place. So for example, if $n = 123$, then $a = 1$, $b = 2$, and $c = 3$."

- a is one of $0, 1, 2, 3, 4, 5, 6, 7, 8, 9$

- b is one of $0, 1, 2, 3, 4, 5, 6, 7, 8, 9$

- c is one of $0, 1, 2, 3, 4, 5, 6, 7, 8, 9$

Me   "So are you comfortable representing n as $100a + 10b + c$?"

Yuri   "Got it!"

1.5 From Ideas to Math

Me   "This is good practice for representing mathematical objects as statements."

Yuri   "What's a mathematical object?"

Me   "It's just a fancy name for a mathematical *something*, like an integer that has some value 0 or higher, but less than 1000. When you're writing a proof, you'll want to write ideas like that as a mathematical expression. 'Integer n such that $0 \leqslant n < 1000$,' for example. Then I took that a step further, and used a, b, c to represent the number as $100a + 10b + c$."

Mathematical Object   **Mathematical Expression**

an integer that's
at least 0, but ⟶
less than 1000

$n = 100a + 10b + c$

$0 \leqslant n < 1000$

Yuri   "It still feels like you're just making a simple thing more complex."

Me   "Sure, all these letters will be confusing if you aren't sure what they represent. But if you take the time to understand what they're doing, there's nothing to be afraid of."

Yuri   "Who said anything about being afraid? It just looks like too much work."

Me   "Not if you have a good reason for doing things that way."

Yuri   "Then hurry up and show me what that good reason is. You were going to prove something, right?"

Me   "Moving on, then. The next thing I wanted to do was add the digits of the number, and call their sum A_n. Do you see how to do that?"

Yuri   "Nothing hard there. You just write $A_n = a + b + c$."

The sum of the digits in n can be written as

$$A_n = a + b + c.$$

Me   "Exactly. Since we set things up so that a, b, c will be the digits in the number, all we have to do is add those three variables to find the sum of the digits in n."

Yuri   "So get to the part where you explain why we did all that."

Me   "Okay, but first let me write a summary of what we've done."

What we have so far

We wrote an integer n (where $0 \leqslant n < 1000$) as

$$n = 100a + 10b + c.$$

We named the sum of n's digits A_n, so

$$A_n = a + b + c.$$

Yuri   "No problem there."

Me   "And here's what we want to prove."

What we want to prove

Let n be an integer, with $0 \leqslant n < 1000$ (i.e., $n = 0, 1, 2, \ldots, 998, 999$). Let A_n be the sum of the digits in n.
Then the following are true:

(1) If A_n is a multiple of 3, then n is a multiple of 3.

(2) If A_n is not a multiple of 3, then n is not a multiple of 3.

Yuri   "So prove it already."

1.6 THE POWER OF MATHEMATICAL STATEMENTS

Me   "Things will be easier if we rewrite what we want to prove as mathematical statements."

What we want to prove, rewritten

(1) If $a + b + c$ is a multiple of 3, then $100a + 10b + c$ is a multiple of 3.

(2) If $a + b + c$ is not a multiple of 3, then $100a + 10b + c$ is not a multiple of 3.

Yuri   "You just replaced the A_n's with $a + b + c$, and the n's with $100a + 10b + c$, right?"

Me   "Right. Now that everything is sorted out, let's try yanking out all the multiples of 3 that we can."

Yuri   "What do you mean, yank them out?"

Me   "I mean doing this."

$$100a + 10b + c = 99a + a + 10b + c \qquad \text{rewrite } 100a \text{ as } 99a + a$$
$$= 3 \times 33a + a + 10b + c \qquad \text{rewrite } 99a \text{ as } 3 \times 33a$$
$$= 3 \times 33a + a + 9b + b + c \qquad \text{rewrite } 10b \text{ as } 9b + b$$
$$= 3 \times 33a + a + 3 \times 3b + b + c \qquad \text{rewrite } 9b \text{ as } 3 \times 3b$$
$$= 3 \times 33a + 3 \times 3b + a + b + c \qquad \text{change order of addition}$$
$$= 3 \times (33a + 3b) + a + b + c \qquad \text{factor out a 3}$$
$$100a + 10b + c = 3 \times (33a + 3b) + a + b + c \qquad \text{the final result}$$

Me   "Whatcha think?"

Yuri   "What *is* this mess? Why write $100a$ as $3 \times 33a + a$?"

Me   "Like I said, I want to yank out all the factors of 3 that I can."

Yuri   "But why do you want to do that?"

Me   "Just look at the final form of the equation."

$$100a + 10b + c = 3 \times (33a + 3b) + a + b + c$$

Yuri   "What am I looking for?"

Me   "Uh, maybe it will be easier to see if I change the order of things."

$$100a + 10b + c = a + b + c + 3 \times (33a + 3b)$$

Yuri   "Or maybe not."

Me   "Do you see how this $3 \times (33a + 3b)$ part here is a multiple of 3?"

Yuri   "Sure, because it's something that's being multiplied by 3."

Me   "Well that means the right side of this equation is $a + b + c$, plus some multiple of 3."

$$100a + 10b + c = a + b + c + \underbrace{3 \times (33a + 3b)}_{\text{a multiple of 3}}$$

Yuri	"And?"
Me	"And, like we said before, if you add a multiple of 3 to some number, if that number was a multiple of 3 then the result will be another multiple of 3. If it wasn't, then the result can't be a multiple of 3. So this equation says that whether or not $100a + 10b + c$ is a multiple of 3 depends on whether $a + b + c$ is a multiple of 3."
Yuri	"Which is what we were aiming for."
Me	"Yep, and that completes the proof. We now know for sure that if you want to see if a number is a multiple of 3, you just have to check if the sum of its digits is a multiple of 3."

What we proved

Let n be an integer, with $0 \leqslant n < 1000$ (i.e., $n = 0, 1, 2, \ldots, 998, 999$). Let A_n be the sum of the digits in n.
Then the following are true:

① If A_n is a multiple of 3, then n is a multiple of 3.

② If A_n is not a multiple of 3, then n is not a multiple of 3.

Me	"We've only proved this works for numbers less than 1000, but we can generalize things further. Here's where the math gets really fun. First, we—"
Yuri	"Whoa, hold up there."
Me	"What's wrong?"
Yuri	"I can follow the proof. I see the logic and all, at least. But something still isn't quite clicking."
Me	"Something in particular?"

Yuri   "That thing about adding 3 to a number, and whether the result is a multiple of 3 depending on the first number. That feels, I dunno, kinda weak."

Me   "Ah, good point. Okay, let's make it click!" ·

1.7 REMAINDERS

Me   "I think this is what's bothering you, written out precisely."

Yuri's question

Let n be a nonnegative integer ($n = 0, 1, 2, 3, \ldots$). Then,

  ① If n is a multiple of 3, then the sum of n and a multiple of 3 is a multiple of 3.

  ② If n is not a multiple of 3, then the sum of n and a multiple of 3 is not a multiple of 3.

Yuri   "Yeah, I think that covers it. It makes sense, I guess, but still..."

Me   "It will make more sense if you think about remainders after dividing by three."

Yuri   "How does that help?"

Me   "If you divide an integer by 3, there are three possible remainders: 0, 1, or 2."

Yuri   "A remainder of 0? That would be no remainder, right? Like, the number was evenly divisible by 3."

Me   "Yeah, sure. But the important thing is that there are three possibilities."

Yuri   "Okay."

Me   "Think about it like this."

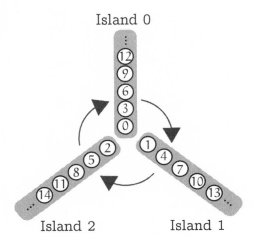

Yuri   "What on earth is this?"

Me   "Imagine we have three islands, Island 0, Island 1, and Island 2. You put the nonnegative integers on those islands according to these rules."

- Integers that leave a remainder of 0 after division by 3 go onto Island 0.

- Integers that leave a remainder of 1 after division by 3 go onto Island 1.

- Integers that leave a remainder of 2 after division by 3 go onto Island 2.

Me   "So 0 goes to Island 0, 1 goes to Island 1, and 2 goes to Island 2, right?"

Yuri   "Sure, I see that."

Me   "So where does 3 go, since there's no Island 3?"

Yuri	"To Island 0, of course, since dividing 3 by 3 doesn't leave a remainder."
Me	"Yep. And 4 goes to Island 1, 5 goes to Island 2, 6 goes to—"
Yuri	"Enough already, I get it. They go around and around, right? Every time you add 1 you move on to the next island."
Me	"That's right, you move around in the direction of the arrows. So what happens when you add 3 to a number?"
Yuri	"Um...I guess you don't get anywhere. Because adding 3 means you end up on the same island you started from."
Me	"And that answers your question."
Yuri	"It does? Hey, it does! Because if you started on Island 0, where all the multiples of 3 are, then you'll just stay there. Same for the other islands, which don't have any multiples of 3!"
Me	"Exactly. And adding a multiple of 3 means you're just adding 3 a certain number of times, so it's the same thing."
Yuri	"That clicking sound you just heard was me *totally* getting this. Okay, I'm absolutely convinced."
Me	"Great! Now we're up to speed on the proof we did for numbers less than 1000. So like I said, the real fun comes when we generalize to—"
Yuri	"Whoa, hold up."

1.8 Yuri's Proposal

Yuri   "So about this method for checking if a number is a multiple of 3 ..."

Me   "What about it?"

Yuri   "I think I found an easier way, without messing around with all the a's and b's and all that."

Me   "This should be interesting."

Yuri   "You add all the digits to do the check, right?"

Me   "Yeah, sure."

Yuri   "Well, 0 is a multiple of 3, so just go adding 1s, and you get multiple, not-a-multiple, not-a-multiple, multiple, not-a-multiple, not-a-multiple, like that."

Me   "You lost me."

Yuri   "Okay, I'll go slower for you. We know 0 is a multiple of 3, right?"

Me   "Yes, it is."

Yuri   "And 1 is not a multiple of 3."

Me   "Correct."

Yuri   "And 2 isn't a multiple of 3 either."

Me   "It is not."

Yuri   "So 0, 1, 2 goes multiple, not-a-multiple, not-a-multiple, yeah?"

Me   "Oh, what you want to say is that we hit a multiple of 3 on every third number?"

Yuri   "That's what I *am* saying!"

$$0 \quad 1 \quad 2 \quad 3 \quad 4 \quad 5 \quad 6 \quad 7 \quad 8 \quad 9 \quad 10 \quad 11 \quad 12$$

Every third number is a multiple of 3

Me   "Well that's neat I guess, but we're talking about ways to check for—"

Yuri   "That's what this is! Pay attention! All the multiples of 3 come every third number. But when you're adding, everything's cool up to 9. The only difference is if you're adding to just the ones digit, or if you're adding to the tens digit, too. Get it?"

Me   "Sorry, Yuri. I'm still lost."

Yuri   "Ugh! Why don't you get this? Are you being dense on purpose?"

Yuri seems close to tears. I bite my lip and proceed carefully.

1.9 YURI'S EXPLANATION

Me   "Hey, Yuri. Let's give it one more shot, a little slower this time."

Yuri glares at me, making me worry that I've lost her, but she finally continues.

Yuri   "I'm thinking in turn from 0."

Me   "Okay, from 0 then."

Yuri   "It works for 0, right?"

Me   "Uh...what works?"

Yuri   "Gah! If you're checking numbers to see if they're multiples of 3 by adding digits and seeing if that gives you a multiple of 3, that works when the number you're checking is 0, right?"

Me   "If $n = 0$ then $A_n = 0$, and both are multiples of 3, so
          sure, that works."

Yuri   "So start from 0 and go up one at a time, through
          $1, 2, 3, 4, 5, 6, 7, 8, 9$. When you do that, A_n and n both
          increase by 1 each time, right? So if A_n is a multiple of
          3 then n will be too, because $A_n = n$ the whole way."

Me   "I see that, yeah."

Yuri   "So the only thing you have to worry about is when you
          move up a digit. You've just got to make sure everything
          works then."

Me   "When you move up a digit?"

Yuri   "When you add 1 to a 9 somewhere."

Me   "Ah hah! I'm starting to see where you're heading."

Yuri   "Then the 9 becomes a 0, and the next unit up gets a 1
          added to it, right?"

Me   "It does indeed."

Yuri   "Well that means the sum of all the digits is having 9
          taken out of it, then 1 added!"

Me   "Okay, I think I'm following you, but let me make sure.
          You're saying that if you add 1 to n, and doing that
          results in two digits being changed, then the effect on
          the sum of the digits is to subtract 9, then add 1. Like,
          if $n = 129$ then $A_n = 1 + 2 + 9 = 12$. When you add 1
          to n it becomes 130, so A_n becomes $1 + 3 + 0 = 4$. And
          that 4 is the same thing you get from subtracting 9 from
          the first A_n, which was 12, then adding 1."

Yuri   "Yes! Exactly!"

Me   "So as an equation it looks something like this."

$$A_{n+1} = A_n - 9 + 1 \qquad \text{the effect of two digits changing}$$

Yuri   "Uh...yeah, that's it."

Me   "What about when more than two digits change, like
            when you add 1 to 99 and get 100?"

Yuri   "You subtract 9 for each 0 that popped up, then add
            1. So you end up subtracting some multiple of 9, and
            adding 1 at the end, right?"

Me   "Wow, Yuri, this is good. So let's see...When you add
            1 to n, you're subtracting some multiple of 9 from the
            sum of n's digits, and adding 1. As an equation, that
            looks like this."

$$A_{n+1} = A_n - 9m + 1 \qquad m \text{ is the number of 0s that appear}$$
$$(m = 0, 1, 2, \ldots)$$

Yuri   "But subtracting a multiple of 9 means you're subtract-
            ing a multiple of 3. On the picture you drew, that means
            you're just spinning backwards around the three islands
            some number of times before you end up back where you
            started."

Me   "Because 9 is a multiple of 3. Yeah, you're right."

Yuri   "So even when more than one digit changes, the effect is
            the same as if just one digit increased by 1. And *that*
            means that if $n + 1$ is a multiple of 3, then A_{n+1} is too,
            and if $n + 1$ isn't, then A_{n+1} isn't either."

            Yuri sits back, glowing with self-satisfaction.

Me   "This is really cool, Yuri."

Yuri   "Isn't it?"

Yuri's discovery

As you increase n in order from $0, 1, 2, \ldots$, either both n and
the sum of its digits A_n will be multiples of 3, or they both
won't.

Me	"By the way, you can use the same kind of method to check for multiples of 9."
Yuri	"Yeah, we did that one in class, too."
Me	"You did?"
Yuri	"Sure. You're talking about adding the digits in a multiple of 9, and seeing if that gives a multiple of 9, right?"
Me	"Right. And what you discovered here made me realize why that works—because when other digits change it's the same as subtracting 9 and adding 1 to the sum of the digits, just like in this problem."
Yuri	"Feel free to call me when you need more math mysteries solved."
Me	"Hey, wait a second—"

My mom calls from the dining room.

Mom	"You kids want some cookies?"
Yuri	"We're on our way!"
Me	"But I—"
Yuri	"Didn't you hear? *Cookies!*"

I kept thinking as Yuri dragged me down the hall. The methods for checking for multiplicity by 3 and 9 were definitely related to Yuri's discovery, because 3 and 9 both divide 9 evenly. But what's so special about 9?

Of course! It's because we count in decimal, in base-10! So couldn't we generalize that to base-n? Couldn't we create a rule for determining if numbers in base-n were multiples of $n - 1$, using this "subtracting $n - 1$ and adding 1" pattern?

" ... but if you don't understand how rules work, you'll never be able to improve them."

Problems for Chapter 1

Problem 1-1 (Checking for multiples of 3)

Which of (a), (b), and (c) are multiples of 3?

(a) 123456

(b) 199991

(c) 111111

(Answer on page 187)

Problem 1-2 (Representation as mathematical statements)

Let n be an even integer in the range $0 \leqslant n < 1000$. Letting a, b, c respectively be the hundreds, tens, and ones digits of n, what values can a, b, c take?

(Answer on page 188)

Problem 1-3 (Building a table)

In this chapter, the narrator used A_n to represent the sum of the digits in an integer n. For example, when $n = 316$,

$$A_{316} = 3 + 1 + 6 = 10.$$

Using that, fill in the blanks in the following table:

n	0	1	2	3	4	5	6	7	8	9
A_n										

n	10	11	12	13	14	15	16	17	18	19
A_n										

n	20	21	22	23	24	25	26	27	28	29
A_n										

n	30	31	32	33	34	35	36	37	38	39
A_n										

n	40	41	42	43	44	45	46	47	48	49
A_n										

n	50	51	52	53	54	55	56	57	58	59
A_n										

n	60	61	62	63	64	65	66	67	68	69
A_n										

n	70	71	72	73	74	75	76	77	78	79
A_n										

n	80	81	82	83	84	85	86	87	88	89
A_n										

n	90	91	92	93	94	95	96	97	98	99
A_n										

n	100	101	102	103	104	105	106	107	108	109
A_n										

(Answer on page 189)

CHAPTER 2

Prime Numbers

"Can you make a donut without
making a donut hole?"

2.1 THE SIEVE OF ERATOSTHENES

I went to the library after class, and found Tetra staring intently at
a book.

Me   "Hey, Tetra. What're you so deep into?"

Tetra   "Something that you might like, actually."

Me   "Must be math, then."

Tetra   "Good guess! It's about something called the Sieve of
          Eratosthenes. Heard of it?"

Me   "Isn't that a way to find prime numbers?"

Tetra   "So you *have* heard of it. Go figure."

Me   "Well, it's pretty famous. It's hard to read about primes
          and not stumble across it."

Tetra   "I didn't realize it was such a big deal."

Me   "It's an important concept, but I don't remember it being
          particularly hard."

Tetra   "This book doesn't really say much about it.   Just
          that Eratosthenes was a very wise person in ancient
          Greece, and that he figured out how to...uh...'reveal
          the primes by successively eliminating multiples.' Then
          there's this big chart with a bunch of numbers."

          I sit next to Tetra and look at the book.

Me   "Yeah, I remember this now. It's pretty easy to get,
          maybe with a simpler explanation. Want me to show
          you?"

Tetra   "Please do!"

2.2 Primes and Composites

Me   "So to build the Sieve of Eratosthenes, you—"

Tetra   "Hang on. Before we talk about that, let me make sure
          I'm working with the right definition of a prime number."

Definition of prime number

A *prime number* is an integer greater than 1 with only two
divisors, 1 and itself.

Me   "Sure, that looks right. Can you give some specific ex-
          amples?"

Tetra   "The first one is 2, right? Then 3, and 5, and 7. The
          next one would be...let's see...11, I guess?"

Me   "Well done."

Tetra   "Because the only numbers that evenly divide 2 are 1
         and 2, and the only numbers that evenly divide 3 are 1
         and 3, and the only—"

Me   "Yeah, you've got it down. Also, numbers like 4 and
         9—ones that aren't prime because they *do* have a divi-
         sor other than 1 and themselves—are called composite
         numbers."

Tetra   "Why composite?"

Me   "Because they're *composed* of at least two primes.
         They're the product of multiplying two or more primes
         together."

Definition of composite number

A *composite number* is a number that can be represented as
the product of two or more primes.

Tetra   "I see ... I think."

Me   "The difference is even easier to see if you perform prime
         factorization on numbers larger than 1. If you write them
         as products of primes, in other words."

$2 = 2$ 2 is prime

$3 = 3$ 3 is prime

$4 = 2 \times 2$ 4 is composite (product of primes $2, 2$)

$5 = 5$ 5 is prime

$6 = 2 \times 3$ 6 is composite (product of primes $2, 3$)

$7 = 7$ 7 is prime

$8 = 2 \times 2 \times 2$ 8 is composite (product of primes $2, 2, 2$)

$9 = 3 \times 3$ 9 is composite (product of primes $3, 3$)

$10 = 2 \times 5$ 10 is composite (product of primes $2, 5$)

Tetra	"So you multiply primes together to make composites. Like 2×2 to get 4, and 2×3 to get 6."
Me	"Exactly. So composites will have at least three divisors."

$\underline{2}$ factors of 2 $(1, 2)$ 2 is prime

$\underline{2}$ factors of 3 $(1, 3)$ 3 is prime

$\underline{3}$ factors of 4 $(1, 2, 4)$ 4 is composite

$\underline{2}$ factors of 5 $(1, 5)$ 5 is prime

$\underline{4}$ factors of 6 $(1, 2, 3, 6)$ 6 is composite

$\underline{2}$ factors of 7 $(1, 7)$ 7 is prime

$\underline{4}$ factors of 8 $(1, 2, 4, 8)$ 8 is composite

$\underline{3}$ factors of 9 $(1, 3, 9)$ 9 is composite

$\underline{4}$ factors of 10 $(1, 2, 5, 10)$ 10 is composite

Tetra	"So what's 1? Prime or composite?"
Me	"Neither one."
Tetra	"It's just ... 1?"
Me	"Actually it has its own name—the unit."
Tetra	"Wow, so many words to learn. Prime, composite, unit ... "
Me	"Oh, and don't forget zero. That's not prime, composite, *or* the unit."
Tetra	"What a mess!"
Me	"Let's do some cleaning up, then. It's not so bad with some organization."

Categorizing the natural numbers

Zero	0											
Unit		1										
Prime			2	3		5		7				11	...
Composite					4		6		8	9	10		12	...

Me "That covers everything, I think. So what happens if you start with $0, 1, 2, 3, \ldots$, and take out zero, the unit, and the composites?"

Tetra "Umm... Oh! Only the primes are left!"

Me "And that's exactly what the Sieve of Eratosthenes does. Taking out 0 and 1 is easy enough. The Sieve is a way of weeding out the composites, leaving you with just primes."

Tetra "How, specifically?"

Me "Well, you start with the first prime, 2, and take out all of its multiples. Since they're multiples of 2, they have to be composites, right?"

Tetra "Sure, okay... I guess."

Me "Hmm. How about we do the whole thing, on paper."

Tetra "Excellent idea!"

2.3 BUILDING THE SIEVE

Me "Let's start with a table of numbers up to 99."

0	1	2	3	4	5	6	7	8	9
10	11	12	13	14	15	16	17	18	19
20	21	22	23	24	25	26	27	28	29
30	31	32	33	34	35	36	37	38	39
40	41	42	43	44	45	46	47	48	49
50	51	52	53	54	55	56	57	58	59
60	61	62	63	64	65	66	67	68	69
70	71	72	73	74	75	76	77	78	79
80	81	82	83	84	85	86	87	88	89
90	91	92	93	94	95	96	97	98	99

Integers 0 through 99

Me   "First, get rid of zero and the unit."

Tetra   "Like this, right?"

Got rid of 0 and 1

Me   "Right. Now the smallest number remaining is 2, which
            we know is prime because 1 and itself are its only divi-
            sors, so circle that."

Tetra   "We're going to circle all the primes, right? Okay, done."

We now know 2 is prime

Me   "Now we want to get rid of all the numbers that are
            multiples of 2, except 2 itself."

Tetra   "Okay, so I cross out 4, and 6, and 8, and... oh, I guess
            I can just cross out every other box."

| ⊘ | 1 | ② | 3 | 4 | 5 | 6 | 7 | 8 | 9 |
| 10 | 11 | 12 | 13 | 14 | 15 | 16 | 17 | 18 | 19 |

Knock out other multiples of 2

Me   "Right. What you're crossing out are all the numbers
            that can be evenly divided by 2, right?"

Tetra   "... $20, 22, 24, 26, \ldots$"

Me   "Uh, Tetra?"

Tetra   "... $28, 30, 32, \ldots$"

Me   "Tetra!"

Tetra   "Huh? What?"

Me   "You're crossing out all the numbers that can be evenly
            divided by 2, right?"

Tetra   "Right."

Me   "And a number that can be evenly divided by 2 has 2 as
            a factor, right?"

Tetra   "Yeah, sure."

Me   "So when you cross out all the multiples of 2, you're
            getting rid of all the composite numbers that have 2 as
            a factor."

Tetra   "Yep. Let me get back to you in a minute, though. I
            have some more crossing out to do."

		②	3		5		7		9
	11		13		15		17		19
	21		23		25		27		29
	31		33		35		37		39
	41		43		45		47		49
	51		53		55		57		59
	61		63		65		67		69
	71		73		75		77		79
	81		83		85		87		89
	91		93		95		97		99

Multiples of 2 greater than 2 are crossed out

Tetra   "Okay, done! All the multiples of 2 are gone. Well, except for 2 itself."

Me   "Good. Now the smallest number left is 3, so it must be our next prime."

Tetra   "How does being the smallest number make it prime?"

Me   "Well, other than 1 and itself, the only other potential factor is 2, right?"

Tetra   "Sure."

Me   "But 3 stuck around after we removed all the multiples of 2, so it can't be a multiple."

Tetra   "Oh, that makes sense."

Me   "And since 3 can't be a multiple of 2, 2 in turn can't be a factor of 3. So 3 must be prime."

Tetra   "Congratulations, 3, you're officially a prime number!"

Tetra circles the 3 with a flourish.

We now know 3 is prime

Me   "So now we can go ahead and knock off all the numbers greater than 3 that are multiples—6, 9, 12, 15 and so on."

Tetra   "Okay, here goes! Wait, 6 is already crossed off."

Me   "Because it was a multiple of 2, right?"

Tetra   "Oh, of course. I'm going to cross it off again, anyway."

Multiples of 3 greater than 3 are crossed out

Me   "Come to think of it, all the numbers you hit that are already crossed off will be a multiple of 6, since they're a multiple of both 2 and 3."

Tetra   "Oh, neat! And...that's all the multiples of 3."

Me   "So what's the next number that's still around?"

0	1	②	③	4	5	6	7	8	9
10	11	12	13	14	15	16	17	18	19
20	21	22	23	24	25	26	27	28	29
30	31	32	33	34	35	36	37	38	39
40	41	42	43	44	45	46	47	48	49
50	51	52	53	54	55	56	57	58	59
60	61	62	63	64	65	66	67	68	69
70	71	72	73	74	75	76	77	78	79
80	81	82	83	84	85	86	87	88	89
90	91	92	93	94	95	96	97	98	99

Multiples of 2 and 3 are crossed out

Tetra   "The smallest number we haven't crossed off is . . . 5."

Me   "Right, because 5 isn't a multiple of either 2 or 3."

Tetra   "Which means its only factors are 1 and 5, so it's prime!"

Me   "You're getting the hang of this. I guess you could think of 4 as another candidate factor, but it got crossed off when we did multiples of 2. If 4 was a factor of 5, that would mean 5 was a multiple of 4, so it would have been crossed out along with 4. So we know for sure that 1 and 5 are the only factors of 5."

Tetra   "So I guess I get to circle 5, and cross out its multiples. Let's see . . . 10, 15, 20, 25 . . . Look, I'm going down two columns!"

0	1	②	3	4	⑤	6	7	8	9
10	11	12	13	14	15	16	17	18	19
20	21	22	23	24	25	26	27	28	29

5 is prime, so cross out other multiples of 5

Me   "That's because there are 10 columns in the table, and 5 evenly divides 10."

Tetra   "Okay, done. That's all of them, up to 95."

0̸	1̸	②	③	4̸	⑤	6̸	7	8̸	9̸
1̸0̸	11	1̸2̸	13	1̸4̸	1̸5̸	1̸6̸	17	1̸8̸	19
2̸0̸	2̸1̸	2̸2̸	23	2̸4̸	2̸5̸	2̸6̸	2̸7̸	2̸8̸	29
3̸0̸	31	3̸2̸	3̸3̸	3̸4̸	3̸5̸	3̸6̸	37	3̸8̸	3̸9̸
4̸0̸	41	4̸2̸	43	4̸4̸	4̸5̸	4̸6̸	47	4̸8̸	49
5̸0̸	5̸1̸	5̸2̸	53	5̸4̸	5̸5̸	56	5̸7̸	5̸8̸	59
6̸0̸	61	6̸2̸	6̸3̸	6̸4̸	6̸5̸	6̸6̸	67	6̸8̸	6̸9̸
7̸0̸	71	7̸2̸	73	7̸4̸	7̸5̸	7̸6̸	77	7̸8̸	79
8̸0̸	8̸1̸	8̸2̸	83	8̸4̸	8̸5̸	8̸6̸	8̸7̸	8̸8̸	89
9̸0̸	91	9̸2̸	9̸3̸	9̸4̸	9̸5̸	9̸6̸	97	9̸8̸	9̸9̸

Multiples of 5 are crossed out

Me   "So the next prime is...?"

Tetra   "7! Watch out, multiples of 7, here I come!"

Crossed out multiples of 7, too

Me   "And next is 11 ..."

Tetra   "This is fun! Look at all the primes popping out!
          $2, 3, 5, 7, 11, \ldots$ Huh, that's weird."

Me   "What?"

Tetra   "$22, 33, 44, 55, 66, 77, 88, 99, \ldots$ All the multiples of 11 are
          already crossed out! What a weird coincidence!"

All multiples of 11 are already gone

2.4 A COINCIDENCE?

Me   "That's no coincidence. It's because $11^2 > 99$."

$$11^2 = 11 \times 11 = 121 > 99$$

Tetra   "What does that have to do with it?"

Me   "The multiples of 11 greater than 11 itself are $11 \times 2, 11 \times 3, 11 \times 4, \ldots$, right?"

Tetra   "Sure."

Me   "But 11×2 is a multiple of 2, 11×3 is a multiple of 3, 11×4 is a multiple of 4, and so on."

Tetra   "Which means . . . ?"

Me   "Well, a multiple of 11 will be in the form $11 \times n$, meaning it's a multiple of both 11 and n. You've already crossed out all the multiples of 2, 3, 5, and 7, and circled 11. That means every number less than 11 has either been circled, or crossed out."

Tetra   "Yeah, I see that."

Me   "So if there are any multiples of 11 that aren't crossed out yet, they'd be in the form $11 \times n$, where n is some number greater than 11. Because we've already looked at all the numbers less than 11."

Tetra   "I get it! 11 times some number greater than 11 would be bigger than 11×11, which is already 121 and too big to be in the table!"

$$11 \times n > 11 \times 11 = 121$$

Me   "Exactly. And that's why you won't find any multiples of 11 in this table that aren't already crossed out."

Tetra   "Doesn't that also mean we're done? There can't be any more numbers to cross out, can there?"

Me   "That's right. Every number left in the table must be a
            prime."

Tetra   "Circles galore!"

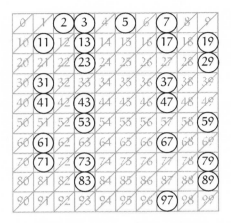

After 11, all remaining numbers must be prime

Me   "And that's it. You've used the Sieve of Eratosthenes to
            find the primes. All the primes 99 or less, at least"

Tetra   "Yay!"

Me   "Here, let me write a summary."

Finding primes using the Sieve of Eratosthenes

You can find all primes less than a natural number N by the following algorithm:

Step 1. Create a table of numbers from 0 to N, and cross out zero (0) and the unit (1).

Step 2. If any numbers are left, circle the smallest remaining number, p. If no numbers are left, stop. (The circled number p is a prime number.)

Step 3. Cross out all multiples of prime p larger than p, and repeat **Step 2.** (The numbers you crossed out have p as a factor.)

When you're done, all primes in the table will be circled, and zero, the unit, and all composite numbers will be crossed out.

Tetra   "That was fun! Filter out the 2s, filter out the 3s, filter out the 5s... Oh! Oh!"

Me   "Oh what?"

Tetra   "I get it! It *is* a sieve!"

Me   "Come again?"

Tetra   "Hang on a sec..."

> Tetra opens her notebook and starts drawing a large graph. After sketching for a while, she looks up, blinking.

Tetra   "Check it out! A sieve!"

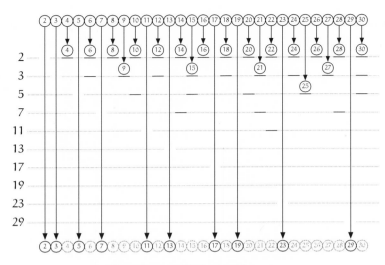

The Sieve of Eratosthenes

Tetra	"I kept wondering why it was called a sieve, but here it is. It's a sieve made out of numbers! Layers and layers of numbers that only the primes can drop down through!"
Me	"What am I looking at here?"
Tetra	"See? All the multiples of 2 get hung up in the 2 layer. Then all the multiples of 3 that aren't multiples of 2 get hung up in the 3 layer."
Me	"Huh. Yep, there they are. $9, 15, 21, 27 \ldots$"
Tetra	"Then all the multiples of 5 that aren't multiples of 2 or 3 get hung up in the 5 layer, and so on and so on. Every prime you find makes a new layer in the sieve!"
Me	"This is one of the coolest graphs I've ever seen..."
Tetra	"You can also see that thing about 11 here."
Me	"What thing about 11?"

Tetra   "About how everything left over after we get to 11 has to be prime, since $11 \times 11 > 99$. Except this graph only goes up to 30, so in this case it's 7. Because $7 \times 7 = 49$, which is greater than 30, right? That's why no numbers are being caught by the 7 sieve! Everything's already been caught!"

Me   "Wow, Tetra. You're amazing. I just love this."

Tetra   "I ... uh ... Thanks."

Tetra looks down, blushing.

Tetra   "Anyway, I totally get this now, how you can use the Sieve of Eratosthenes to filter out composite numbers and find the primes. But ... "

Me   "Something bothering you?"

Tetra   "It just seems like there should be, I dunno, a more *direct* way of finding primes."

Me   "What do you mean, direct?"

Tetra   "Isn't there some method that doesn't involve just chipping away everything that *isn't* a prime? Some way of pulling out the primes themselves?"

Me   "Now that's an interesting question. And my honest answer is ... I don't know."

Miruka   "What are you guys up to?"

2.5 MIRUKA

Tetra   "Hey, Miruka! Perfect timing!"

Miruka pushes her glasses up her nose, and squints at my table of primes.

Miruka   "The Sieve of Eratosthenes, huh?"

Tetra   "Feels like I'm the last person in the world to learn about it."

Miruka   "Why'd you arrange them like that?"

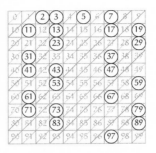

Table of primes

Me   "Huh? Did I do something wrong?"

Miruka   "Just curious. Why do it this way?"

Me   "I ... uh ... No real reason. Do I need one?"

Miruka   "Tetra, how do you normally arrange the natural numbers?"

Tetra   "I just write them all in a row, I guess."

Primes in a row

Miruka   "That works, too."

Tetra   "Can't fit many on a page that way, though."

Me   "Yeah, you've got to break them somewhere if you want to play with a lot of them."

Miruka   "Doesn't mean you have to use ten per row, though."

Me   "Maybe we should make two columns, like this?"

Primes in rows of 2

Tetra   "Neat! When you do it this way, all the primes except 2 are in the right column!"

Me   "Because all the primes except 2 are odd."

Tetra   "Oh, right. I wonder if there isn't some way to arrange the numbers that makes the primes pop out."

Miruka   "What say we go looking?"

Tetra   "Looking for what?"

Miruka   "Patterns in the primes."

2.6 Searching for Patterns

Miruka commandeers the notebook. Tetra and I move to either side of her.

Miruka   "Let's start by lining up zero and the unit."

Me   "You're starting out just like I did!"

Miruka   "But you went down from here. I want to move up."

Tetra   "*Up?*"

Me   "Up above the 1? Not the 0?"

Miruka   "If I did that I'd just be recreating your table, only upside down."

Me   "I suppose so, yeah."

Tetra   "Where to next?"

Miruka   "Left for the 3."

Tetra   "Then up for the 4, right?"

Miruka   "No. Left again."

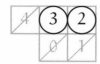

Tetra   "But now you're sticking out over the edge."

Me   "I guess you'll go up for the 5?"

Miruka   "Nope. Down this time."

Me   "I'm so confused."

Tetra   "Oh, she's making rows! Next is left, right?"

Miruka   "Down."

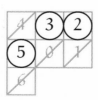

Tetra   "Hmm ... right, up, left, left, down, down ..."

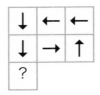

Me   "Dragon Whirlwind Kick from Street Brawlers IV!"

Miruka and Tetra give me an icy stare.

Tetra   "I get it! You're going around in circles!"

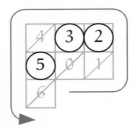

Miruka   "Score one for Tetra."

Me   "So 7, 8, 9 go right?"

Miruka   "They do."

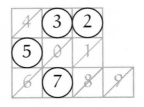

Tetra   "Then 10, 11, 12 go up?"

Miruka   "Yep."

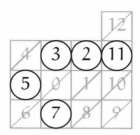

Me   "I'm not seeing where you're going with this, though. What's up?"

Miruka   "Do you really want me to tell you, or do you want to figure it out for yourself?"

Me   "Sorry, sorry. Carry on."

Tetra   "Next we go left until we hit... 16, right?"

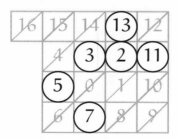

Me   "Then down to 20."

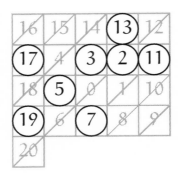

Tetra   "And right to 25 . . . Oh! Oh! Oh!"

Tetra raises her right hand and waves furiously.

Me   "What? What?"

Miruka   "She found it."

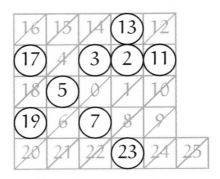

What did she find?

2.7 A DISCOVERY?

Tetra   "An X! There's an X!"

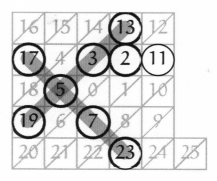

Are the primes forming an X?

Me   "That's because the primes other than 2 are all odd, so they're—Uh, no. It's not that simple, is it."

Miruka   "Let's go on to 30."

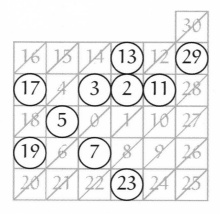

Tetra   "See? See? 31 is prime!"

Me   "Huh. It's like it had to be."

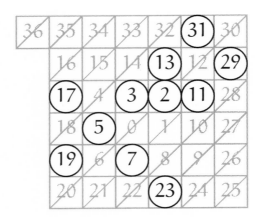

Tetra   "Maybe it's not an X, but there's definitely two diagonal
             lines there.   The $19, 5, 3, 13, 31$ one and the $17, 5, 7, 23$
             one."

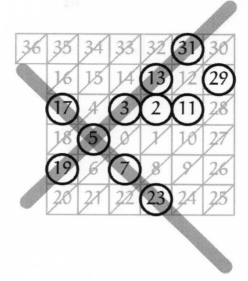

Are the primes forming diagonals?

Me "I dunno. Could still be a coincidence."

Miruka "Well let's go up to 81 and see what happens."

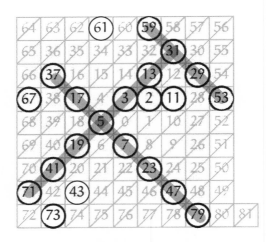

Curled around to 81

Tetra	"Aww... 57 and 65 let us down. C'mon, guys, you're supposed to be primes!"
Me	"I've gotta say, I was kind of rooting for them too."
Miruka	"Let's stop at 99 for now."

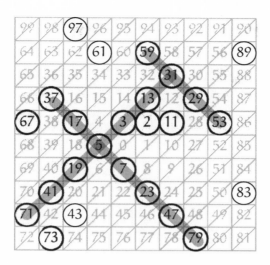

Primes seem to like to form diagonals

Tetra   "Still lots of diagonal action going on here."

Miruka   "There is. Isn't it curious, how arranging the natural numbers in a spiral like this seems to line up so many primes?"

Miruka pushes her glasses up her nose.

Tetra   "Yeah, why didn't we see anything like this when we used the Sieve of Eratosthenes? Why do the primes seem to be making patterns in this spirally thing?"

2.8 THE ULAM SPIRAL

Miruka   "This 'spirally thing' has a name, actually: the Ulam spiral."

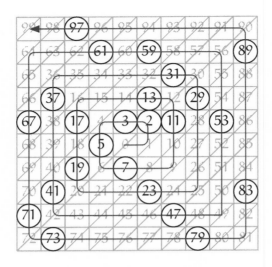

The Ulam spiral

Tetra   "What's an Ulam?"

Miruka   "Ulam is a mathematician. He discovered this by doodling during a boring lecture."

Tetra   "I'll bet finding this woke him up."

Me   "I would have been jumping up and down in my seat."

Tetra   "So what happens after this, if you just keep going around and around?"

         Miruka digs around in her backpack for a while, then slaps a photocopy on the table.

Miruka   "*This* is what happens."

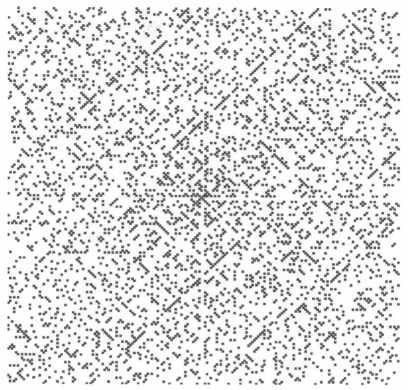

The Ulam spiral, extended

Tetra   "Whoa! It looks kind of random at first, but look at all the diagonals! There's some horizontal lines, too!"

Me   "This is amazing."

Tetra   "Now this is why I like graphs. I don't know what's going on here, but I can tell at a glance that *something* is!"

2.9 EULER

Me   "With this much regularity, doesn't it seem like you could represent this as an equation somehow?"

Miruka   "You aren't the first to ask that question. In fact, there are some known equations that can produce lots of primes. Euler found a good polynomial like that in 1772.

$$n^2 - n + 41$$

Legendre found a very similar polynomial. So similar, in fact, that these are often both attributed to Euler."

$$P(n) = n^2 + n + 41$$

Tetra   "So you can just use these to find all the primes?"

Miruka   "I said lots of primes, not all of them. As in, there are lots of values for n that will give you a prime."

Tetra   "Ooh, let me try! Let's see... $P(0)$ would be $0^2 + 0 + 41$, which gives you 41, which is a prime all right!"

Me   "And $P(1) = 1^2 + 1 + 41 = 43$, another prime."

Tetra   "Let's keep going!"

Values for $P(n) = n^2 + n + 41$

n	$P(n)$		n	$P(n)$		n	$P(n)$		n	$P(n)$	
0	41	prime	25	691	prime	50	2591	prime	75	5741	prime
1	43	prime	26	743	prime	51	2693	prime	76	5893	composite
2	47	prime	27	797	prime	52	2797	prime	77	6047	prime
3	53	prime	28	853	prime	53	2903	prime	78	6203	prime
4	61	prime	29	911	prime	54	3011	prime	79	6361	prime
5	71	prime	30	971	prime	55	3121	prime	80	6521	prime
6	83	prime	31	1033	prime	56	3233	composite	81	6683	composite
7	97	prime	32	1097	prime	57	3347	prime	82	6847	composite
8	113	prime	33	1163	prime	58	3463	prime	83	7013	prime
9	131	prime	34	1231	prime	59	3581	prime	84	7181	composite
10	151	prime	35	1301	prime	60	3701	prime	85	7351	prime
11	173	prime	36	1373	prime	61	3823	prime	86	7523	prime
12	197	prime	37	1447	prime	62	3947	prime	87	7697	composite
13	223	prime	38	1523	prime	63	4073	prime	88	7873	prime
14	251	prime	39	1601	prime	64	4201	prime	89	8051	composite
15	281	prime	40	1681	composite	65	4331	composite	90	8231	prime
16	313	prime	41	1763	composite	66	4463	prime	91	8413	composite
17	347	prime	42	1847	prime	67	4597	prime	92	8597	prime
18	383	prime	43	1933	prime	68	4733	prime	93	8783	prime
19	421	prime	44	2021	composite	69	4871	prime	94	8971	prime
20	461	prime	45	2111	prime	70	5011	prime	95	9161	prime
21	503	prime	46	2203	prime	71	5153	prime	96	9353	composite
22	547	prime	47	2297	prime	72	5297	prime	97	9547	prime
23	593	prime	48	2393	prime	73	5443	prime	98	9743	prime
24	641	prime	49	2491	composite	74	5591	prime	99	9941	prime

Tetra   "You're right! It *does* give a lot of primes!"

Miruka   "It's very interesting to overlay the primes this function
             generates onto the Ulam Spiral."

Miruka digs into her backpack again and pulls out
another photocopy.

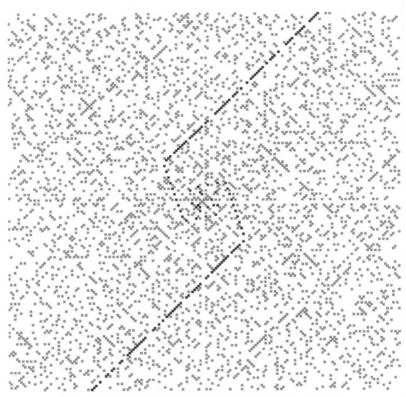

The Ulam spiral, with primes generated by
$P(n) = n^2 + n + 41$ overlaid

Tetra   "So many primes for such a short equation!"

Me   "These darker points are the primes generated by this
             $P(n)$, right? Wow, look how they line up like that. No
             way this just happens by chance."

Miruka "There's a reason for it, if you want to take a swim in the deep waters of number theory."

Me "Uh, maybe some other day."

Miruka "Then here's the short version: none of the values produced by this function are divisible by 2, 3, 5, or 7."

Me "Whoa. Maybe I want to see a proof after all."

Miruka "Then first we have to—"

Ms. Mizutani "The library is *closed!*"

Our school librarian's announcement brought a sudden end to our math talk. It was time to head home and do some thinking for ourselves.[1]

"Can you make a donut hole without creating a donut?"

---

[1] Credit: Much of the discussion in this chapter follows David Wells's *Prime Numbers: The Most Mysterious Figures in Math* (Wiley, 1986).

Problems for Chapter 2

Problem 2-1 (Primes)

Which of the following statements are mathematically accurate?

(a) 91 is a prime number.

(b) The sum of two primes is an even number.

(c) If an integer 2 or greater is not a composite number, then it is a prime number.

(d) All primes have exactly two factors.

(e) All composite numbers have three or more factors.

(Answer on page 191)

Problem 2-2 (The Sieve of Eratosthenes)

Use the Sieve of Eratosthenes to find all prime numbers less than 200.

(Answer on page 193)

Problem 2-3 (Improving the Sieve of Eratosthenes)

The algorithm for the Sieve of Eratosthenes on p. 41 doesn't account for the fact that you can quit once $p^2 > N$. Improve the algorithm so that it takes advantage of this.

(Answer on page 194)

Problem 2-4 (The binomial $n^2 + n + 41$)

Prove that the binomial $P(n) = n^2 + n + 41$ results in an odd number for all integer values of $n \geqslant 0$.

(Answer on page 195)

CHAPTER 3

Number Guessing and Mysterious 31

"When can you always guess a number someone is thinking of?"

3.1 THE NUMBER GUESSING TRICK

Yuri   "Close your eyes!"

Me   "Why?"

Yuri   "When a beautiful girl tells you to close your eyes, you don't ask questions."

Me   "When that happens, I'll— *Ouch!* Okay, okay! They're closed."

Yuri   "Done! You can open your eyes now!"

16 17 18 19	8 9 10 11	4 5 6 7	2 3 6 7	1 3 5 7
20 21 22 23	12 13 14 15	12 13 14 15	10 11 14 15	9 11 13 15
24 25 26 27	24 25 26 27	20 21 22 23	18 19 22 23	17 19 21 23
28 29 30 31	28 29 30 31	28 29 30 31	26 27 30 31	25 27 29 31

Me   "What's with the cards?"

Yuri   "Prepare to be astounded, as The Amazing Yuri performs
            the mystifying Number Guessing Trick!"

Me   "I don't think real magicians announce tricks like that."

Yuri   "Just shut up and watch."

Me   "Yes ma'am. But why did I have to close my eyes?"

Yuri   "It builds suspense."

Me   "If you say so. I take it you're going to guess some num-
            bers?"

Yuri   "Very astute of you."

The Number Guessing Trick

This trick can predict your favorite day of the year. First,
think of the day only, ignoring the month. For example, if
your favorite day of the year is

- February 14, use 14

- If it's March 16, use 16

- If it's December 24, use 24

Next, leave each of the five cards that contains your number
face up, and flip over each of the cards that does *not* contain
your number.

16 17 18 19	8 9 10 11	4 5 6 7	2 3 6 7	1 3 5 7
20 21 22 23	12 13 14 15	12 13 14 15	10 11 14 15	9 11 13 15
24 25 26 27	24 25 26 27	20 21 22 23	18 19 22 23	17 19 21 23
28 29 30 31	28 29 30 31	28 29 30 31	26 27 30 31	25 27 29 31

Me   "I hate to spoil the mood, but—"

Yuri   "Silence, as The Amazing Yuri predicts the future! I'm
          getting a vision of you saying 'I know how this trick
          works.'"

Me   "I know how this trick works."

          Yuri gives an exaggerated sigh.

Yuri   "Even when you know the trick, etiquette demands you
          fake it and pretend to be surprised. This is *exactly* why
          you don't have a girlfriend."

Me   "Fine, I'll pretend to be surprised then. By all means,
          amaze me."

3.2 YURI'S PERFORMANCE

Yuri   "Do you have your number? Don't tell me! Just think
          it."

Me   "Yes. I'm thinking of a number between 1 and 31."

Yuri   "Well then, good sir, flip over all the cards that don't
          have your number in them."

Me   "That would be... these three."

What number did he choose?

Yuri   "Indeed? Then the number you are thinking of must be
          none other than... 12!"

Me   "Yep."

Yuri	"Gah! We've been over this! You're supposed to say something like 'Wow, Yuri! How'd you know!?'"
Me	"Wow, Yuri. How'd you know?"
Yuri	"I really hate you sometimes."
Me	"Yeah, yeah. Let me give it a shot. Think of a number."
Yuri	"Wait, you can do it, too?"
Me	"Like I said, I know how this trick works."

3.3 MY PERFORMANCE

Yuri	"Okay, I've got one. Go ahead."
Me	"And now, madame, flip over the cards that don't have your number."
Yuri	"Just these two."

16 17 18 19		4 5 6 7		1 3 5 7
20 21 22 23		12 13 14 15		9 11 13 15
24 25 26 27		20 21 22 23		17 19 21 23
28 29 30 31		28 29 30 31		25 27 29 31

What number did she choose?

Me	"Then your number must be . . . 21!"
Yuri	"Yep."
Me	"What was all that about magic trick etiquette?"

Yuri smiles and shrugs.

3.4 How the Trick Works

Me   "What's cool about this trick is how simple it is."

Yuri   "Yeah, all you have to do is add the upper left numbers of each card."

How to 'guess' the number

Adding the numbers in the upper left corner of each face-up card gives the correct answer.

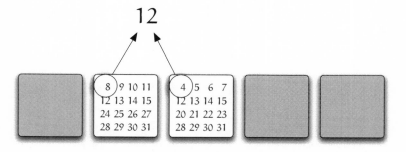

The cards when 12 was chosen

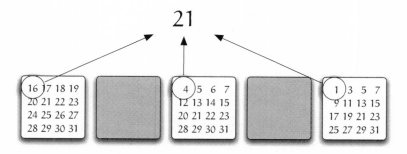

The cards when 21 was chosen

Me   "Makes it so easy that anyone could do it, really."

Yuri   "Did you just insult me?"

Me   "Not intentionally. Do you know why the trick works,
            by the way?"

Yuri   "Like I said, you just add the numbers."

Me   "That's how you do the trick, not why it works."

Yuri   "Same difference."

Me   "Not at all. What I want to know is, why does adding
            the upper left numbers give you the answer?"

Yuri   "Because the cards are designed that way, doofus."

Me   "Look at it this way. Say you lost these cards, but wanted
            to do the trick again. Could you make a new set your-
            self?"

16 17 18 19	8 9 10 11	4 5 6 7	2 3 6 7	1 3 5 7
20 21 22 23	12 13 14 15	12 13 14 15	10 11 14 15	9 11 13 15
24 25 26 27	24 25 26 27	20 21 22 23	18 19 22 23	17 19 21 23
28 29 30 31	28 29 30 31	28 29 30 31	26 27 30 31	25 27 29 31

Could you create your own set of cards?

Yuri   "Well, maybe not by myself. But I *could* just buy an-
            other copy of the magazine that these came with."

Me   "So that's where you got them. Anyway, the reason you
            couldn't create your own is because you don't know why
            the trick works. You sure you want to remain ignorant?"

Yuri   "There you go, pushing my buttons."

Me   "Let's look a bit deeper and figure out how you could
            make your own cards. Maybe even a better version."

Yuri   "Better how?"

Me   "Well, for example these cards only work for numbers 1 through 31. Once we know why the trick works, maybe we could create a set that can handle bigger numbers."

Yuri   "Huh...I thought the 1 through 31 thing was from the number of days in a month."

Me   "That was just added on after the fact, by whoever made the trick. The 31 is special for another reason, which you would know if you looked deeper into what's going on."

Yuri   "Okay, you've got me. Show me how it works."

Me   "No fun if I just tell you. Let's see what you can figure out for yourself."

Yuri   "Even better."

3.5 GUESSING NUMBERS 1 THROUGH 1

Me   "Let's start small. Instead of 1 to 31, let's say you're going to guess a number from 1 to 1."

Yuri   "Won't exactly make for a spectacular performance."

Me   "Just go with it. To do this trick, you don't need five cards, right? Just one, like this."

A card for guessing 1 to 1

Yuri   "I'm not convinced I'd need cards at all."

Me   "Stick with me. The point is, you just need this one card, with a 1 on it. I can only guess 1, so I leave the card face up."

Yuri   "What a dumb trick."

Me   "But it isn't dumb to start with extreme examples. It's
              pretty important, in fact."

Yuri   "Whatever you say."

3.6 GUESSING NUMBERS 1 THROUGH 2

Me   "So now can you make cards for guessing a number 1
              through 2."

Yuri   "Ah, so *that's* where you're going with this. We're going
              to keep adding cards."

Me   "Yup."

Yuri   "So something like this, I guess?"

Cards for guessing 1 to 2

Me   "Exactly. You just need a card with a 1 on it, and one
              with a 2."

Yuri   "So I'm not really guessing the number, you're just show-
              ing it to me."

Me   "Well isn't that what this whole trick is about?"

Yuri   "Mmm...maybe. I guess 1 through 3 is next?"

3.7 GUESSING NUMBERS 1 THROUGH 3

Me   "Do you see how to make the cards?"

Yuri   "All I've got to do is make you show me the answer again. Like this."

Three cards for guessing 1 to 3

Me   "That works, sure, but here's where you can start making it look like a magic trick."

Yuri   "How's that?"

Me   "By still only using two cards."

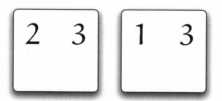

Just two cards for guessing 1 to 3

Me   "One card should have 2 and 3, the other one 1 and 3."

Yuri   "Oh, right! Here's where the adding starts!"

Me   "Yep. For example if I was thinking of 3, I would leave both cards face up."

Yuri   "And I would just add the 2 and the 1 to get the answer."

Me   "Right. Here's all the possibilities."

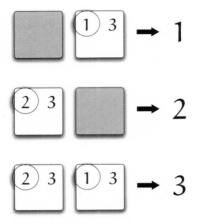

Face up cards for guessing 1, 2, **and** 3

Yuri   "So I'm still making you tell me what the answer is."

Me   "An excellent observation! I'm giving you the answer right off if I'm thinking of 1 or 2. But even if I'm thinking of 3 I have to leave both cards face up, and it's easy enough to just add 1 and 2."

Yuri   "I'm starting to see how this works, but I'm not quite there yet."

Me   "You'll get that feeling a lot, just before you make a big discovery."

Yuri   "Keep going, then. On to 1 through 4?"

Me   "Let's give it a shot."

3.8 GUESSING NUMBERS 1 THROUGH 4

Yuri   "So we have to add another card now? We've flipped just the two every way they can be flipped."

Me   "That's right. There are only four possible ways, and
          we've used them all."

Yuri   "Four? I only see three."

Me   "We haven't talked about it, but I could have turned
          both cards face down."

Yuri   "And how am I supposed to read numbers if you do
          that?"

Me   "You don't—that would be the case where I didn't think
          of a number. Let's call that case 'zero.'"

Yuri   "Why zero?"

Me   "Because it's like adding nothing at all. There's no num-
          bers to add, right?"

Yuri   "Okay, I guess we can go with that."

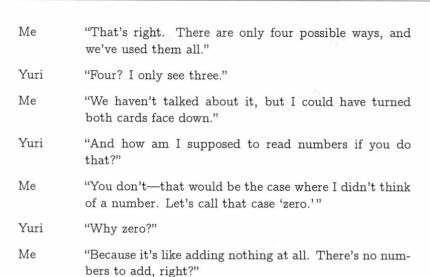
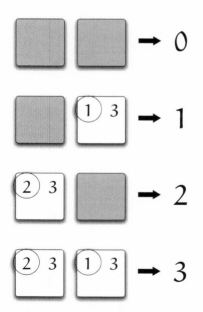

The four ways of choosing two cards

Me   "If it helps, think of the trick as being about guessing a
          number from 0 to 3. We used up all four card patterns
          to do that, so to extend the trick to 4, we need to add
          another card."

Yuri   "And I guess it just has to have a 4 on it, like this?"

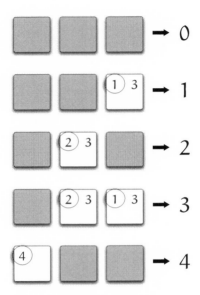

Cards for guessing 0 to 4

Yuri   "Wait, that's not all I can do. I can add the 4 and the 1
          to get 5. And 4 and 2 to get 6!"

Me   "And?"

Yuri   "Huh?...Oh, and 4, 2, and 1 to get 7!"

Me   "Good eye! But what's still missing?"

Yuri   "Duh, I have to add numbers to get you to flip the right
          cards. Let's see...Add a 5 to the 4 card, and a 1 to the
          5 card. No, wait. I need a 6 on the 4 card...Yikes, this
          is getting messy."

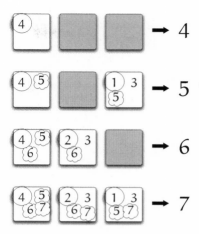

The cards for guessing 0 to 4 can also handle 5, 6, 7

Me   "No worries, you're getting there."

Yuri   "Okay, done. Now I can guess any number you're thinking of, from 0 to 7, using these three cards."

Me   "Here, let me write all the possibilities."

Yuri   "You chill. I've got this."

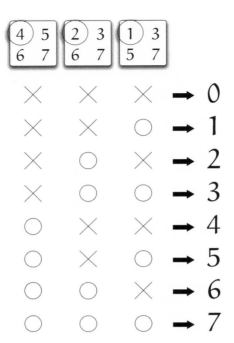

Representing 0 to 7 with three cards (circles show face-up cards, crosses show face-down cards)

Me   "You're getting the hang of this."

Yuri   "Hmm ... All the numbers on the right card are odd. Does that mean something?"

Me   "You tell me."

Yuri   "Well, it means that card will be face up anytime you're thinking of an odd number. See how the column under it repeats cross, circle, cross, circle?"

Me   "Yet another discovery."

Yuri   "Oh, there's more! The column under the middle card
            has pairs of crosses and circles. And the one on the left
            is in groups of four!"

Me   "Looks like you've found an important pattern."

Yuri   "Important how?"

Me   "Patterns are important because they let you make pre-
            dictions, like 'if this is this, then that must be that.'
            They also lead to discovering regularity."

3.9 FOUR CARDS

Me   "Speaking of discoveries, we found that three cards can
            represent numbers from 0 to 7. So what happens when
            you have four cards?"

Yuri   "What do you mean, what happens?"

Me   "I mean what can you represent now? Can you make a
            list of all the ways of flipping four cards? I want to see
            what happens to that leftmost card."

Yuri   "Well since we're talking about making predictions, I'll
            predict that the top half will be crosses and the bottom
            half will be circles. And I guess we'll have 16 ways of
            arranging the cards, since that's twice 8?"

Me   "Interesting. Let's see how The Amazing Yuri's powers
            of precognition pan out. Start with just the possible
            patterns. We'll worry about the numbers on the cards
            later."

Yuri   "Okay, here goes."

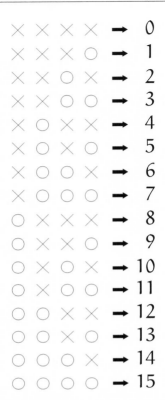

**Representing 0 to 15 with four cards (circles show face-up
cards, crosses show face-down cards)**

Me   "Wow, that was fast."

Yuri   "It's all about the patterns. Now we just have to write
          the numbers that each card has a circle for. Hang on."

          Sunlight flashes off Yuri's ponytail as she furiously
          writes strings of numbers.

Yuri   "Done!"

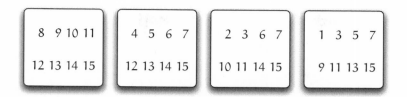

Cards for guessing 0 to 15

Me   "Notice something interesting about these numbers?"

Yuri   "What am I supposed to be noticing here?"

Me   "You just made these cards yourself, right?"

Yuri   "Yeah, so?"

Me   "Look at the cards you brought with you. You've just duplicated half the numbers on them."

Yuri   "Well whaddaya know."

16 17 18 19	8 9 10 11	4 5 6 7	2 3 6 7	1 3 5 7
20 21 22 23	12 13 14 15	12 13 14 15	10 11 14 15	9 11 13 15
24 25 26 27	24 25 26 27	20 21 22 23	18 19 22 23	17 19 21 23
28 29 30 31	28 29 30 31	28 29 30 31	26 27 30 31	25 27 29 31

| 8 9 10 11 | 4 5 6 7 | 2 3 6 7 | 1 3 5 7 |
| 12 13 14 15 | 12 13 14 15 | 10 11 14 15 | 9 11 13 15 |

3.10 RIGHT ON THE MONEY

Me   "We haven't even talked about why the trick works yet, but it's already kinda interesting, isn't it?"

Yuri	"Gotta admit, this is way cooler than just knowing how to do the trick. I didn't really pay any attention to the numbers on the cards before."
Me	"And now?"
Yuri	"I noticed there's only odd numbers on the rightmost card, for one thing. And it's starting to look like there's other patterns."
Me	"That's one of the advantages of writing things out for yourself—you notice things like that."
Yuri	"Oh, also that adding just one card lets you guess a whole lot more numbers."
Me	"That's right. We could only guess from among four numbers with two cards, but adding just one more card lets us use eight numbers, and another card doubled the number of possible answers again."
Yuri	"There's something that feels...I dunno...*just right* about that."
Me	"What do you mean?"
Yuri	"Well, when we use three cards we can guess numbers from 0 to 7, right?"
Me	"Yeah."
Yuri	"And that's all we can do, because we've used up all the cross-and-circle patterns. It's like...like everything fits just right, or something. Umm, I'm not sure how to put this in words."
Me	"No need, I know what you mean. You're talking about a one-to-one correspondence with subsets."
Yuri	"Not quite the words I was searching for."

Me   "You just didn't know them yet. The reason you can guess eight numbers using three cards is because there are eight subsets of a three-element set. In other words, eight ways of choosing the cards."

Yuri   "Flipping them up or down, you mean."

Me   "Right. You've assigned numbers to each up–down pattern, so that every pattern has a number, and every number has its own pattern. I think that's the 'fitting just right' you were talking about. A situation like that is called a one-to-one correspondence, or a bijection if you want to be fancy."

Yuri   "Ugh... I'm turning into a math nerd."

Me   "But you've gotta admit, it's amazing what you can discover just from starting with something as simple as guessing numbers from 1 to 1."

Yuri   "You got me there."

Me   "That's why it's important to start from the obvious."

Yuri   "Where's all this taking us next?"

Me   "How about figuring out the why behind the how in this trick, and what those numbers in the upper left corner are."

Yuri   "Sounds like a plan."

3.11 0 TO 31

Me   "Here's a table we can use to associate all the possible patterns of five cards with the numbers 0 through 31."

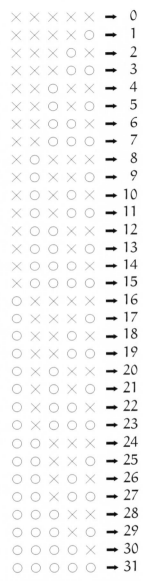

Representing 0 to 31 using 5 cards (circles show face-up
cards, crosses show face-down cards)

Me	"We can use the card patterns in this table to represent each integer 0 through 31."
Yuri	"Patterns on the left, numbers on the right."
Me	"Actually, once you see how to do it you don't even need the table. You can just go straight from number to pattern."
Yuri	"I can figure that out from looking at the cards."
Me	"You don't even need the cards. You just need to do a bit of research on that number in the upper left."
Yuri	"Ooh, I'm doing research now. I feel so smart."

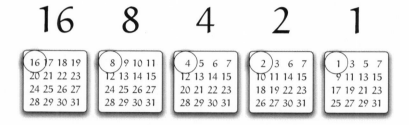

Numbers added in the number-guessing trick

Me	"Tell me, what kind of numbers are these?"

$$16 \quad 8 \quad 4 \quad 2 \quad 1$$

Yuri	"Even ones. No, wait, there's a 1 there."
Me	"More important is that they're powers of 2."

3.12 Powers of 2

Yuri	"What's a power of 2?"
Me	"A number you can get by multiplying 2s together. When you multiply n twos, you write that 2^n."

Powers of 2

$$16 \ = \ \underbrace{2 \times 2 \times 2 \times 2}_{4 \text{ twos}} \ = \ 2^4$$

$$8 \ = \ \underbrace{2 \times 2 \times 2}_{3 \text{ twos}} \ = \ 2^3$$

$$4 \ = \ \underbrace{2 \times 2}_{2 \text{ twos}} \ = \ 2^2$$

$$2 \ = \ \underbrace{2}_{1 \text{ two}} \ = \ 2^1$$

Yuri   "But there's a 1 on this card, too."

Me   "We define the 0th power of 2 as 1."

Yuri   "What do you mean, define it?"

Me   "We just say that's the way things are."

$$1 = 2^0$$

Yuri   "That looks really strange."

Me   "I'm stickin' to it anyway. If you want, you can think of it as multiplying 0 twos together. Maybe sticking some 1s in there will help."

$$16 \ = \ 1 \times 2 \times 2 \times 2 \times 2 \ = 2^4 \quad \text{(Multiply 4 twos)}$$
$$8 \ = \ 1 \times 2 \times 2 \times 2 \ = 2^3 \quad \text{(Multiply 3 twos)}$$
$$4 \ = \ 1 \times 2 \times 2 \ = 2^2 \quad \text{(Multiply 2 twos)}$$
$$2 \ = \ 1 \times 2 \ = 2^1 \quad \text{(Multiply 1 twos)}$$
$$1 \ = \ 1 \ = 2^0 \quad \text{(Multiply 0 twos)}$$

Yuri   "Okay, I'm convinced."

Me   "Good, because these powers of 2 are the secret behind
            your trick."

Yuri   "How?"

Me   "Because you can add combinations of 16, 8, 4, 2, and 1 to
            get any integer from 0 to 31. You can also go backwards,
            from one of those numbers to the pattern we need the
            cards to be in."

Yuri   "Show me."

3.13 Repeated Division

Me   "All we have to do is divide and find remainders, over
            and over. That tells you if a card should be face up or
            face down."

Yuri   "What on earth does division have to do with anything?"

Me   "Watch. Let's try it with, say, 21. Divide 21 by 2^4—
            in other words 16—and you get a quotient of 1 with a
            remainder of 5."

Yuri   "Quotient . . . that sounds so familiar."

Me   "The answer to a division problem, ignoring any remain-
            ders."

Yuri   "Ah, yes, it's coming back to me now."

Me   "Anyway, dividing 21 by 16 give you 1 with a remainder
            of 5, right?"

$$21 \div 16 = 1 \text{ remainder } 5$$

Yuri   "It does."

Me   "Next we take the remainder, and divide it by 8. Divide
            the remainder of that by 4, then repeat with 2 and 1.
            See what's happening with the quotients?"

$$21 \div 16 = \boxed{1} \cdots 5$$

$$5 \div 8 = \boxed{0} \cdots 5$$

$$5 \div 4 = \boxed{1} \cdots 1$$

$$1 \div 2 = \boxed{0} \cdots 1$$

$$1 \div 1 = \boxed{1} \cdots 0$$

Yuri   "Uh...no?"

Me   "Read them off, top to bottom."

Yuri   "$1, 0, 1, 0, 1$."

Me   "That's the pattern we're after. This means to represent
        21, the cards should be up, down, up, down, up."

1 and 0 correspond to "up" and "down" (21 shown here)

Yuri   "So *that's* what you mean by all that going from numbers
        to cards stuff. I wanna try!"

Me   "Then give 12 a shot."

$$12 \div 16 = \boxed{0} \cdots 12$$

$$12 \div 8 = \boxed{1} \cdots 4$$

$$4 \div 4 = \boxed{1} \cdots 0$$

$$0 \div 2 = \boxed{0} \cdots 0$$

$$0 \div 1 = \boxed{0} \cdots 0$$

Me   "Well?"

Yuri   "Umm...$0, 1, 1, 0, 0$ means down, up, up, down, down, so...it worked!"

1 and 0 correspond to "up" and "down" (12 shown here)

Me   "Pretty cool, huh?"

Yuri   "Totally cool! But why does it work? How do the quotients know how the cards should be flipped?"

Me   "If you get a quotient of 1 after dividing by 16, that means there's a 16 in the number that you could pull out. The remainder is what's left after you've subtracted the 16."

Yuri   "Hmm..."

Me   "So dividing by 16, 8, 4, 2, 1 in turn is like saying, 'Is there a 16 in there? How about an 8? Or a 4?' and so on."

Yuri   "Okay, I think I've got this. But you're explaining it wrong."

Me   "How should I be explaining it?"

Yuri   "With alligators."

3.14 Alligator Math

Yuri   "Alligators, chomping on numbers."

Me   "Oh, this is gonna be good."

Yuri   "They have different-sized mouths, and only eat in powers of 2. Here, draw that for me. Gimme five alligators, with mouths sized 16, 8, 4, 2, and 1."

Me   "Something like this?"

$$2^4 = 16$$

$$2^3 = 8$$

$$2^2 = 4$$

$$2^1 = 2$$

$$2^0 = 1$$

Alligators with power-of-2 mouths

Yuri   "I said *alligators*, not ... whatever these things are."

Me   "Gimme a break. It's just a sketch."

Yuri   "What are these dots supposed to be? Eyes? Nose holes?"

Me   "Just tell me how you wanted to feed them."

Yuri   "Oh, right. So the biggest alligator gets to eat first, then passes any leftovers down to the next-biggest one. But these are really picky alligators, and they'll only eat if they can get a full mouthful of food. Anything less than that, they pass on. Like, if you feed them 21, only the 16 and the 4 and the 1 alligators will take a bite."

Me   "Like this?"

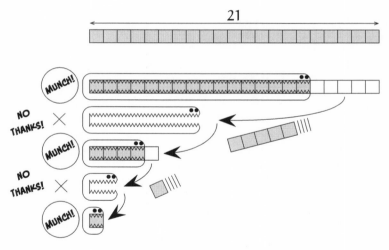

Alligators eating a 21

Yuri   "Right! And if you know which alligators ate, you can figure out what they started out with. Like, if the 16 and the 4 and the 1 alligators look like they're full, then they must have eaten a 21."

$$16 + 4 + 1 = 21$$

Me   "Not how I would put it, but you've obviously got this
            stuff down."

Yuri   "One more! Let's feed them a 12. Then the 8 and the 4
            alligators get to eat."

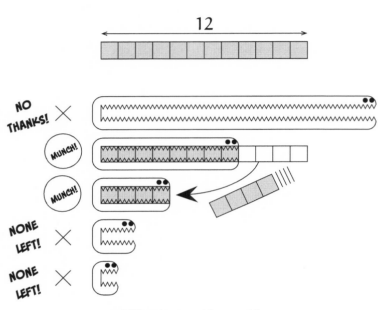

Alligators eating a 12

Me   "I'm starting to like these little guys."

Yuri   "If only they didn't look so goofy."

3.15 MYSTERIOUS 31

Me   "Hey, we can use these alligators to explain the mystery
            of 31."

Yuri   "What mystery?"

Me   "Remember how your number guessing trick used five
            cards to guess a number between 0 and 31?"

Yuri   "Yeah."

Me   "Well, why 31?"

Yuri   "Oh! Because that's the most that five alligators can gobble down at one sitting!"

Me   "Right. Which means if I'm thinking of 31, I'll have to turn all the cards face up."

$$31 = 16 + 8 + 4 + 2 + 1$$

Me   "Here's another way to write that."

$$31 = 2^5 - 1$$

Yuri   "Where did that come from?"

Me   "You can't represent a 32 with five cards, because $32 = 2 \times 2 \times 2 \times 2 \times 2 = 2^5$. You'd have to have a *sixth* card, one with a 32 in the upper left corner. So I'm pulling back one from that by subtracting a 1 from 2^5, to show the largest number you can represent with five cards."

Yuri   "Easier to just say 'five cards can only show numbers up to 31.'"

Me   "But just having that 31 sitting there doesn't tell you much. When you write it like $2^5 - 1$, you can use that 5 to see how many cards you need. Even better, you can generalize and say that with n cards your trick can guess numbers up to $2^n - 1$. Here's a few more."

$$2^1 - 1 = 1 \qquad \text{Max. number with 1 card}$$

$$2^2 - 1 = 3 \qquad \text{Max. number with 2 cards}$$

$$2^3 - 1 = 7 \qquad \text{Max. number with 3 cards}$$

$$2^4 - 1 = 15 \qquad \text{Max. number with 4 cards}$$

$$2^5 - 1 = 31 \qquad \text{Max. number with 5 cards}$$

$$2^6 - 1 = 63 \qquad \text{Max. number with 6 cards}$$

$$2^7 - 1 = 127 \qquad \text{Max. number with 7 cards}$$

$$2^8 - 1 = 255 \qquad \text{Max. number with 8 cards}$$

$$2^9 - 1 = 511 \qquad \text{Max. number with 9 cards}$$

$$2^{10} - 1 = 1023 \qquad \text{Max. number with 10 cards}$$

$$\vdots$$

$$2^n - 1 = 2^n - 1 \qquad \text{Max. number with } n \text{ cards}$$

Yuri   "All the way up to 1023 with just 10 cards! Wow!"

3.16 FROM 2 TO 10

Me   "Have you learned how we count using powers of 10?"

Yuri   "I may have heard something like that before..."

Me   "Maybe this will refresh your memory."

$$10^0 = 1$$

$$10^1 = 10$$

$$10^2 = 100$$

$$10^3 = 1000$$

$$10^4 = 10000$$

$$\vdots$$

$$10^n = \underbrace{1000\cdots00}_{n \text{ zeros}}$$

Yuri   "One, ten, one hundred, one thousand... The powers of ten tell you how many zeros there are."

Me   "Exactly. The way we usually write numbers, each digit is a weighted power of 10. That's called the decimal system, from the word for 'ten' in Latin."

Yuri   "This sounds so familiar, like maybe I dreamed it once."

Me   "Because you were sleeping in math class?"

Yuri   "Very possible."

Me   "Anyway, the decimal system is a way of representing numbers as a sum of powers of ten."

Yuri   "Numbers are addition problems?"

Me   "In a way. Take the decimal number 7038. That's short-hand for 'add seven 1000s, no 100s, three 10s, and eight 1s.'"

$$7038 = \boxed{7} \times 1000 + \boxed{0} \times 100 + \boxed{3} \times 10 + \boxed{8} \times 1$$

Yuri   "I'll stick to the short version."

Me   "You can also write this as powers of 10."

$$7038 = \boxed{7} \times 10^3 + \boxed{0} \times 10^2 + \boxed{3} \times 10^1 + \boxed{8} \times 10^0$$

Yuri   "Still not short enough. And what does this have to do with my trick, anyway?"

Me   "I was getting to that. Your trick works kinda like this, but with weighted powers of 2 instead of 10. You're using binary, in other words."

Yuri   "Explain."

Me   "Well, take the number 12 for example. In binary, you think of that as 'zero 16s, one 8, one 4, zero 2s, and zero 1s.'"

$$12 = \boxed{0} \times 16 + \boxed{1} \times 8 + \boxed{1} \times 4 + \boxed{0} \times 2 + \boxed{0} \times 1$$

Yuri   "0, 1, 1, 0, 0 . . . Same as with the cards!"

Me   "And of course we can do this one using exponents, too."

$$12 = \boxed{0} \times 2^4 + \boxed{1} \times 2^3 + \boxed{1} \times 2^2 + \boxed{0} \times 2^1 + \boxed{0} \times 2^0$$

Yuri   "Right!"

Me   "Decimal and binary use different powers, but see how
            the form of the equation is exactly the same?"

Yuri   "Yeah, sure."

Me   "Decimal numbers are sums of powers of 10, and binary
            numbers are sums of powers of 2. Decimal can use ten
            numbers for its digits, 0 through 9, but binary only uses
            two, 0 and 1. That's why you can use it for your trick."

Yuri   "I don't see the connection."

Me   "Because there's only two sides to the cards. Remember
            how we called a face-down card 0, and a face-up card
            1? We were just replacing the binary 0 and 1 with card
            faces."

Yuri   "Oh, I get it! So the up–down patterns were binary num-
            bers in disguise!"

Me   "Yup. The decimal number 12 is 01100 in binary, so to
            represent that we placed the cards down-up-up-down-
            down."

12 in binary, with 'up' as 1 and 'down' as 0

Yuri   "Sneaky!"

Me   "And *that*, Yuri, is *why* the trick works. Because you're
              making the other person show you the number in bi-
              nary."

Why the trick works

You can 'guess' the number the person is thinking of, because
they've arranged the cards in an up–down pattern that repre-
sents the number in binary notation.

          Mom calls to us from the kitchen.

Mom   "I'm making pancakes! Anyone want some?"

Yuri   "You know I do!"

Yuri and I headed for the dining room, where we stuffed ourselves
like hungry alligators.

"When you can trick them into telling you what the number is."

APPENDIX: NUMBERS IN BINARY AND DECIMAL

00000	0	01000	8	10000	16	11000	24
00001	1	01001	9	10001	17	11001	25
00010	2	01010	10	10010	18	11010	26
00011	3	01011	11	10011	19	11011	27
00100	4	01100	12	10100	20	11100	28
00101	5	01101	13	10101	21	11101	29
00110	6	01110	14	10110	22	11110	30
00111	7	01111	15	10111	23	11111	31

APPENDIX: COUNTING ON YOUR FINGERS IN BINARY

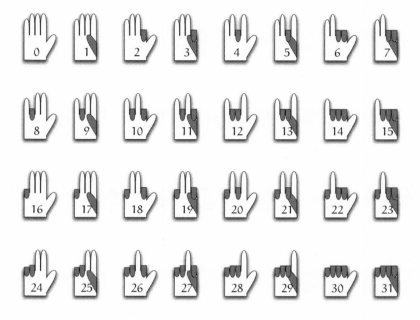

Problems for Chapter 3

Problem 3-1 (Representing numbers with cards)

If you used Yuri's five cards to represent the number 25, what numbers would be in the upper-left corners?

(Answer on page 196)

Problem 3-2 (Numbers on the cards)

What other numbers would be on the card with a 2 in its upper-left corner? (No peeking at the appendix, please!)

$$
\begin{array}{cccc}
2 & ? & ? & ? \\
? & ? & ? & ? \\
? & ? & ? & ? \\
? & ? & ? & ?
\end{array}
$$

(Answer on page 196)

Problem 3-3 (Multiples of 4)

Using Yuri's five cards, think of a way to know at a glance if someone is thinking of a number that's a multiple of 4. Be sure to arrange the cards so that the numbers in the upper-left corner are 16, 8, 4, 2, 1, in that order.

(Answer on page 197)

Problem 3-4 (Flipping cards)

Suppose you've used Yuri's cards to represent some number N. What number would you get if you flipped every card, so that face-up cards became face down, and face-down cards became face-up? Give your answer using N.

(Answer on page 198)

Problem 3-5 (n cards)

Each of Yuri's five cards has sixteen numbers on them. If she instead had n cards, how many numbers would be on each?

(Answer on page 198)

CHAPTER 4

Math on Clocks

"How can you create something you've
never seen?"

4.1 TRUST ISSUES

Yuri   "Close your eyes!"

Me   "Why?"

Yuri   "Do you never learn anything?"

Me   "I've learned to be careful when you're around."

Yuri   *"Close 'em! Now!"*

Me   "All right, all right. They're closed."

4.2 A CLOCK PUZZLE

Yuri   "Okay, you can look now!"

I open my eyes. A box with three dials rests on
the table.

Me	"What's this?"
Yuri	"It's a clock puzzle!"
Me	"These are clocks?"
Yuri	"Well just look at them."
Me	"They don't have minute hands. Or enough numbers."
Yuri	"That's what makes it a puzzle! I call this one on the left the 2-clock."

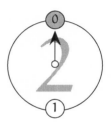

The 2-clock

Me	"And this one in the middle has three numbers, so—"
Yuri	"—that's the 3-clock."

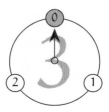

The 3-clock

Me   "So I guess this one on the right is the 5-clock."

Yuri   "Yep! Isn't it cool?"

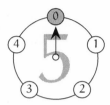

The 5-clock

4.3 OPERATING THE CLOCK PUZZLE

Me   "The clocks aren't moving. How do you use them to tell time?"

Yuri   "They don't tell time. They tell numbers."

Me   "Now things are starting to get interesting."

Yuri   "I figured that would hook you. See the two buttons here?"

Me   "Reset and count?"

RESET   COUNT

The reset and count buttons

Yuri   "Right. When you press the reset button, the hands on all three clocks go to 0 and you start a new puzzle. When all the hands are like that, it's called pattern 000."

The reset button sets all hands to 0
(pattern 000)

Me   "What then?"

Yuri   "You press the count button, and the hands each move
          ahead by one. See?"

Pressing the count button advances each hand by one
(pattern 111)

Yuri   "Are you paying attention? What just happened?"

Me   "Each hand moved forward by one, so all the clocks are
          pointing at 1 now. I guess that's pattern 111?"

Yuri   "It is. So what will happen if you press the count button
          again?"

Me   "I assume each hand will advance by one again."

Yuri   "Well what are you waiting for? Try it!"

**After pressing the count button twice
(pattern 022)**

Me "Just like I said. So this would be pattern 022."

Yuri "So you see that the hand on the 2-clock is back to 0 now? The important thing here is that the numbers don't necessarily get bigger when the hands advance. Okay, ready for a quiz?"

Me "Can I study a little bit first?"

Yuri "Oh, if you must."

Yuri pushes the box my way, and I press the count button.

**After pressing the count button three times
(pattern 103)**

Me "This is kinda fun. Now the 3-clock is back to 0."

I push the button again.

**After pressing the count button four times
(pattern 014)**

Me   "Once more to get the 5-clock back to zero."

**After pressing the count button five times
(pattern 120)**

Yuri   "And it's back."

Me   "Hey, once more will get two of them pointing to 0."

**After pressing the count button six times
(pattern 001)**

Yuri   "Stop there for a minute."

Me   "Why?"

Yuri   "Do you remember how many times you've pressed the button?"

Me   "Six. I've been counting."

4.4 THE CLOCK PUZZLE PROBLEM

Yuri   "Okay, study time is over. Here's your quiz."

The clock puzzle problem

You press the reset button, setting the clock to pattern 000.

Pattern 000

Each time you press the count button, each hand moves forward by one. How many times do you need to press the count button to create pattern 024?

Pattern 024

Yuri   "Oh, and you have to answer without pressing the button any more!"

Me   "Hmm . . . This might take some thinking."

        Yuri grins.

Me   "No button presses at all, huh?"

Yuri   "Not a one."

4.5 Considering the 2-clock

Me   "Okay, let's think this through, taking things in order.
            First, there are three clocks."

Yuri   "There are indeed."

Me   "I'm gonna start with just the 2-clock. With each button
            press, it flips back and forth between 0 and 1."

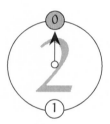

The 2-clock

Yuri   "It does."

Me   "We're after pattern 024, so the 2-clock needs to point
            at 0. That means we have to push the count button an
            even number of times."

- In pattern 024 the 2-clock points to 0, so we have to press the
  count button an even number of times.

Yuri   "Good so far."

Me   "I think that's all we need to know for the 2-clock. On
            to the next one."

4.6 Considering the 3-clock

| Me | "When we press the count button, the 3-clock cycles through $0 \to 1 \to 2 \to 0 \to 1 \to 2 \to \cdots$." |

| Yuri | "Yep." |

| Me | "In pattern 024, the 3-clock is pointing at 2, so if we divide the number of button presses by 3, we should get a remainder of 2." |

| Yuri | "Whoa, where did that come from?" |

| Me | "Because dividing numbers by 3 gives you remainders in the same $0 \to 1 \to 2 \to 0 \to 1 \to 2 \to \cdots$ pattern as the hand on the 3-clock." |

- If you press the button 0 times, the hand points at 0.

- If you press the button 1 times, the hand points at 1.

- If you press the button 2 times, the hand points at 2.

- If you press the button 3 times, the hand points at 0.

- If you press the button 4 times, the hand points at 1.

- If you press the button 5 times, the hand points at 2.

    $\vdots$

| Yuri | "Uh...okay." |

| Me | "See? Divide the number of button presses by 3, and the remainder is the number that the hand is pointing at." |

| Yuri | "What goes on in your brain that makes you look at clocks and think 'remainders'?" |

| Me | "They're closely related." |

Yuri narrows her eyes.

Me   "No, really—problems about things like clocks and calen-
            dars that keep repeating are often solved using remain-
            ders."

Yuri   "If you say so..."

Me   "Look at it this way. When you've pressed the count
            button three times, the 3-clock is pointing back at the
            0, right? That means it will be pointing at 0 on press
            number 3, and on 6, and 9 and 12 and all the other
            multiples of 3. It's like every third press has reset things,
            as if you hadn't pressed the button at all. So really
            there's only three possible situations."

> Press (a multiple of 3) + $\underline{0}$ times   ... the 3-clock points to $\underline{0}$
>
> Press (a multiple of 3) + $\underline{1}$ times   ... the 3-clock points to $\underline{1}$
>
> Press (a multiple of 3) + $\underline{2}$ times   ... the 3-clock points to $\underline{2}$

Yuri   "Okay, I see that."

Me   "We're after pattern 024, where the 3-clock is pointing
            at 2, so we need to press the button a number of times
            that when divided by 3 leaves a remainder of 2."

Yuri   "But it still doesn't tell us how many times to press the
            button!"

Me   "No, but now we have one more clue."

- In pattern 024 the 2-clock points to 0, so we have to press the
  button an even number of times.

- In pattern 024 the 3-clock points to $\underline{2}$, so we have to press the
  button a number of times that, when divided by 3, will leave
  a remainder of $\underline{2}$.

Me   "Actually we can improve our first clue. An even number
            is one that leaves a remainder of 0 when divided by 2,
            right?"

- In pattern 024 the 2-clock points to 0, so we have to press the button a number of times that, when divided by 2, will leave a remainder of 0.

- In pattern 024 the 3-clock points to 2, so we have to press the button a number of times that, when divided by 3, will leave a remainder of 2.

Yuri   "Verrry interesting."

Me   "This is what I mean by taking things in order. There are 3 clocks, so it makes sense to think about them one at a time."

4.7 CONSIDERING THE 5-CLOCK

Me   "We've got a pattern going here, so let's apply it to the 5-clock. That one points to 4 in the 024 pattern, which gives us a third clue."

- In pattern 024 the 2-clock points to 0, so we have to press the button a number of times that, when divided by 2, will leave a remainder of 0.

- In pattern 024 the 3-clock points to 2, so we have to press the button a number of times that, when divided by 3, will leave a remainder of 2.

- In pattern 024 the 5-clock points to 4, so we have to press the button a number of times that, when divided by 5, will leave a remainder of 4.

Yuri   "So what do we do with all these clues?"

4.8 REMAINDER 4 WHEN DIVIDED BY 5

Me   "Now we go looking for the number of button presses. It's easy to find the numbers that leave remainder 4 when divided by 5. That would be 4, 9, 14, 19 and on like that. The number we're after has to be one of those."

$$4, 9, 14, 19, \ldots$$

Yuri   "How'd you just reel those off like that?"

Me   "Well the 4 is easy, right? Because if you divide 4 by 5
            you get 0 with remainder 4."

$$4 \div 5 = 0 \,\text{remainder}\, 4$$

Yuri   "Sure."

Me   "After that you just have to add 5s. Because no matter
            how many 5s you add, you aren't changing the remain-
            der. Remember how we did something like that the other
            day, when we talked about the number islands?"

Yuri   "Oh, yeah! Okay, so we start with 4, then $4 + 5 = 9$, and
            $9 + 5 = 14$, and $14 + 5 = 19$, and ..."

Me   "And so on, right. But check out our first clue—it says
            the number of times we press the button has to be even.
            So the answer has to be 4, or 14, or something bigger
            that fits both rules."

Yuri   "But there are more than two rules!"

Me   "Right, because there's our hint about the 3-clock. That
            says the number of button presses has to leave a remain-
            der of 2 when we divide by 3. So let's check what we
            have so far."

- Dividing 4 by 3 leaves a remainder of 1,
  so that can't be the answer ...

- Dividing 14 by 3 leaves a remainder of 2,
  so that should be the answer!

Yuri   "Whoa!"

Me   "Let's check each hint one more time, just to be sure."

- 14 divided by 2 leaves remainder 0. OK!

- 14 divided by 3 leaves remainder 2. OK!

- 14 divided by 5 leaves remainder 4. OK!

Yuri   "So *that's* how you solve this problem."

Me   "Ah ah ah! Not so fast."

Yuri   "Gah! Here comes another of your 'one more things'..."

Me   "But an important one! Don't think that this is *the* way to do this problem, it's just the way *I* did it. With most math problems there's more than one path to the answer, and if you get to thinking there's one particular way you're 'supposed' to do things, you're really limiting yourself. So tell me how you would do it."

Yuri   "Push the button until 024 came up."

Me   "Oh, come on. Don't just—"

Yuri   "Well who's limiting who now? Huh?"

Me   "Okay, you win. Brute force is a perfectly acceptable answer, I suppose."

Answer to the clock puzzle

Pressing the button 14 times results in the pattern 024.

4.9 COMING BACK AROUND

Yuri   "So your answer is 14, huh? I guess I'll give you partial credit."

Me   "What do you mean? I just showed you how—"

Yuri   "But 14 isn't the *only* answer!"

Me   "Huh?"

Yuri   "Because if you keep pushing that button, eventually the
            clocks will spin back to the 024 pattern again!"

Me   "Hmm . . . Interesting."

Yuri   "Uh oh, now you're going to figure more stuff out, aren't
            you. I should have kept my mouth shut."

Me   "Oh, come on. It'll be fun. We'll define a number of
            button presses giving the 024 pattern as N . . ."

Yuri   "And here come the letters. I knew it."

Me   "Well, it's easier to use 'N' than to keep saying 'a number
            of button presses giving the 024 pattern,' right?"

- N divided by 2 leaves remainder 0. (N is even.)

- N divided by 3 leaves remainder 2.

- N divided by 5 leaves remainder 4.

Yuri   "Let's start with the dividing by 5 one."

Me   "Sure, might as well. So that gives us . . ."

$$4, 9, 14, 19, 24, 29, 34, 39, 44, 49, 54, 59, 64, \ldots$$

Yuri   "They all end in 4s and 9s!"

Me   "But we're only interested in the even ones, remember?"

$$4, 14, 24, 34, 44, 54, 64, \ldots$$

Yuri   "And now they all end in 4."

Me   "Let's comb through those for numbers that leave re-
            mainder 2 when divided by 3."

$$2, 5, 8, 11, 14 \leftarrow \text{found one!}, 17, 20, 23, 26, 29,$$
$$32, 35, 38, 41, 44 \leftarrow \text{found one!}, 47, 50, \ldots$$

Yuri   "See? Told you there would be more than one answer.
            44 works, too, and I'll bet there's even bigger answers
            out there."

Me   "Ugh, and now I realize I've just wasted a bunch of time."

Yuri   "How's that?"

Me   "Because we just had to add 30 to our first answer, 14.
            Like this."

Answer to the clock puzzle (improved)

The minimum number of button presses needed to generate the 024 pattern is 14. Following that, each multiple
of 30 presses will result in another 024 pattern.

$$14, 44, 74, 104, 134, 164, \ldots$$

As a mathematical expression, the number of required
button presses is

$$30n + 14 \qquad (n = 0, 1, 2, 3, \ldots).$$

Yuri   "What's with the 30? Where did that come from?"

Me   "From multiplying 2 and 3 and 5. That gives 30, and
            that means every time you push the button 30 times,
            the dials will return to the position they started from."

Yuri   "How do you know that?"

Me   "Because that's what the numbers tell us. Look."

- The 2-clock points at 0 after every 2 pushes. In other words, it points at 0 after some-multiple-of-2 pushes.

- The 3-clock points at 0 after every 3 pushes. In other words, it points at 0 after some-multiple-of-3 pushes.

- The 5-clock points at 0 after every 5 pushes. In other words, it points at 0 after some-multiple-of-5 pushes.

Yuri   "So?"

Me   "So if the number of pushes is a multiple of 2, *and* it's a multiple of 3, *and* it's a multiple of 5, then all three hands must be pointing to 0."

Yuri   "Oh, yeah—hey, yeah!"

Me   "A number that's a multiple of 2, 3, and 5 is called a common multiple of those numbers. And 30 is the smallest number like that, so it's called the least common multiple."

Yuri   "So you get the least common multiple just by multiplying the numbers?"

Me   "Not necessarily. You'll always get a common multiple that way, but not necessarily the *least* common multiple."

Yuri   "Why'd we get it this time?"

Me   "Because 2, 3, and 5 are all primes."

4.10 USING A TABLE

Yuri   "Too much work."

Me   "What is?"

Yuri   "All this stuff you had to do to get pattern 024. Seems
         like there should be a way to just go like, *bam*, there's
         the answer."

Me   "Always looking for the shortcuts, ain'cha?"

Yuri   "Proves I'm normal."

Me   "Maybe a table would contain the *bam* you're after."

Yuri   "Why a table?"

Me   "Because you could just skim down the patterns to look
         for the one you're after. *Bam*, there it is."

Button presses and resulting patterns

Presses	2-clock	3-clock	5-clock
0	0	0	0
1	1	1	1
2	0	2	2
3	1	0	3
4	0	1	4
5	1	2	0
6	0	0	1
7	1	1	2
8	0	2	3
9	1	0	4
10	0	1	0
11	1	2	1
12	0	0	2
13	1	1	3
⇒ 14	0	2	4
15	1	0	0
16	0	1	1
17	1	2	2
18	0	0	3
19	1	1	4
20	0	2	0
21	1	0	1
22	0	1	2
23	1	2	3
24	0	0	4
25	1	1	0
26	0	2	1
27	1	0	2
28	0	1	3
29	1	2	4
30	0	0	0

Me   "See the last line here? This shows you that everything repeats after 30 presses, so you just have to add 30s to the 14 solution you found up here."

Yuri   "Well now I can read the answer right off, but it's still too much work to make the table in the first place."

Me   "Maybe drawing some lines makes it easier to see the patterns in here."

Button presses and resulting patterns (with lines)

Presses	2-clock	3-clock	5-clock
0	0	0	0
1	1	1	1
2	0	2	2
3	1	0	3
4	0	1	4
5	1	2	0
6	0	0	1
7	1	1	2
8	0	2	3
9	1	0	4
10	0	1	0
11	1	2	1
12	0	0	2
13	1	1	3
14	0	2	4
15	1	0	0
16	0	1	1
17	1	2	2
18	0	0	3
19	1	1	4
20	0	2	0
21	1	0	1
22	0	1	2
23	1	2	3
24	0	0	4
25	1	1	0
26	0	2	1
27	1	0	2
28	0	1	3
29	1	2	4
30	0	0	0

Me   "If you look at this right, you can see the pattern of how the clock hands diverge, then come back to all point at 0 again after 30 button presses."

Yuri   "Neat!"

Me   "See how line 30 is the same as line 0? That means the whole system has returned to where it started at pattern 000. After that it will just repeat itself."

Yuri   "Okay, the table is cool and all. But it still lacks *bam*."

Me   "Well what kind of solution are you looking for?"

Yuri   "Something ... cleaner. A little bit of calculation, maybe, but not all this."

Me   "You're hard to please."

I try to think of other ways to solve the problem, but nothing comes to mind. Everything seems so obvious as to defy further simplification.

Yuri   "Well?"

Me   "Nothing yet."

Yuri   "Maybe I should have gone easy on you, given you a box with just one clock."

Me   "Cute, but— Hey, wait a minute."

Yuri   "Huh?"

Me   "That's a great idea! We'll just use one clock, and create 1s!"

Yuri   "That makes no sense whatsoever."

The clock puzzle problem (review)

You press the reset button, setting the clock to pattern 000.

Pattern 000

Each time you press the count button, each hand moves forward by one. How many times do you need to press the count button to create pattern 024?

Pattern 024

4.11 HOW WE WANT THINGS TO BE

Yuri   "What do you mean, make 1s?"

Me   "Let me back up a bit. What is it that's been making this problem such a pain?"

Yuri   "That there's three clocks to deal with?"

Me   "Exactly. So we can make things a lot simpler if we just talk about one clock instead."

Yuri   "Yeah, but—"

Me   "Bear with me. Say we were only interested in the 5-clock. Then the problem is super simple, right? To get a 4, you just have to press 4 times."

Yuri   "Well, sure."

Me   "And once we've gotten to the 4, then every time we press 5 more times, the clock hand effectively hasn't moved, right? So it's in the same place after 5 presses, and 10 presses, and 15, and so on."

Yuri   "Because it ends up where it started for every multiple of 5. We've been through this. But there isn't just one clock, there's three. You're just saying the problem would be easier if it was easier!"

Yuri crosses her arms with a huff.

Me   "You're right, I am. But that's an important attitude to take when you're doing math."

Yuri   "What are you talking about?"

Me   "Tackling a tricky math problem is like solving a mystery. Simplifying things can get rid of irrelevant details and uncover new clues."

Yuri   "Turning three clocks into one isn't a clue, it's a magic trick."

Me   "Not necessarily ... "

4.12 THREE CLOCKS INTO ONE

Me   "Remember when I was first pushing the button, and you had me stop after six presses?"

Yuri   "Sure. What about it?"

Me   "Let's do that one more time. Here, I'll hit the reset button to get pattern 000. Now six button presses to get pattern 001."

Six button presses from pattern 000 gives pattern 001

Me   "In pattern 001, the 2-clock and the 3-clock both point at 0, and the 5-clock points to 1."

Yuri   "Yeah, so?"

Me   "We know the 2-clock and the 3-clock both spun around before they got back to zero, but let's say we *didn't* know that."

Yuri   "Why would we say that?"

Me   "If you look at pattern 001 that way, isn't it sorta like thinking the 2-clock and the 3-clock aren't moving, and just one clock—the 5-clock—advanced by 1?"

Yuri   "I guess you could look at it that way, sure."

Me   "That's what gave me the idea of using just one clock, and making 1s!"

Yuri   "That still makes absolutely *no* sense."

Me   "Okay, here's how it works. If you press the count button six times, in the end the only change is that the 5-clock has advanced by 1."

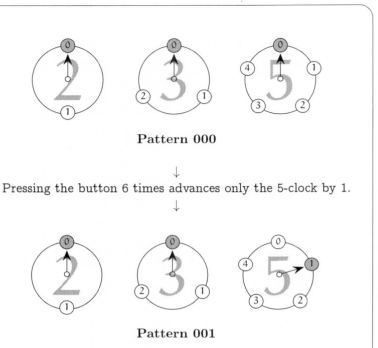

Pattern 000

↓
Pressing the button 6 times advances only the 5-clock by 1.
↓

Pattern 001

Me   "So if you start from pattern 001 and press the button six more times, you end up with pattern 002, right?"

Pattern 001

↓

Pushing the button 6 more times again advances only the
5-clock by 1.

↓

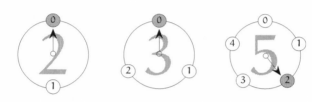

Pattern 002

Yuri   "Ah, I see what you're doing. You're advancing just the 5-clock by pressing the button in groups of six."

Me   "Exactly! And you can do that as many times as you want, to get the 5-clock to point to any number you want, without changing the other clocks."

Yuri   "How is that helpful?"

Me   "Because grouping button presses like this lets us treat the three clocks as just one."

Yuri   "Whoa—hold on."

Me   "See where this is going?"

Yuri   "You're going to do that to each clock, and set them
          separately?"

Me   "I am indeed."

Yuri   "Ha!"

Me   "See how that simplifies things? The puzzle is tricky
          when you think about just one button press at a time,
          because that changes each of the three clocks. That
          makes it harder to get them all in just the place you
          want them to be. Changing the clocks one at a time is
          much simpler. Cool, huh?"

Yuri   "Not so fast. It worked for the 5-clock, but can you do
          that for the other ones, too?"

Me   "Sure. Let's do the 2-clock. We just have to figure out
          how many button presses gives us pattern 100."

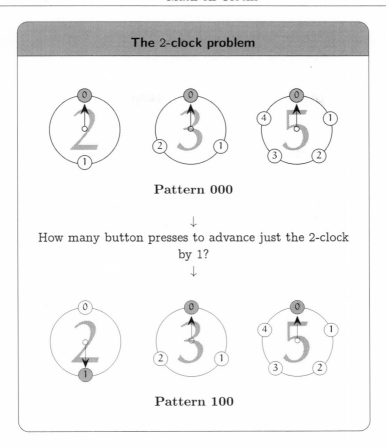

The 2-clock problem

Pattern 000

↓

How many button presses to advance just the 2-clock
by 1?

↓

Pattern 100

Me   "Same thing for the 3-clock. For that one, we want to
            know how many presses take us from 000 to 010."

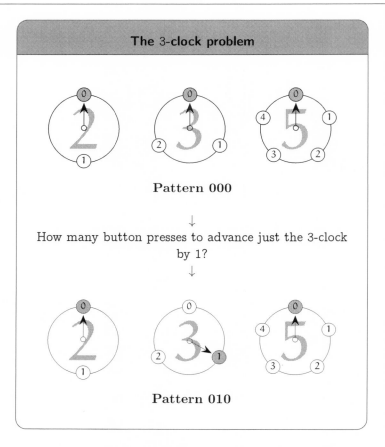

The 3-clock problem

Pattern 000

↓

How many button presses to advance just the 3-clock
by 1?

↓

Pattern 010

Yuri   "So we just need patterns 100, 010, and 001! And we can
              read that right off the table!"

Button presses and resulting patterns

Presses	2-clock	3-clock	5-clock
0	0	0	0
1	1	1	1
2	0	2	2
3	1	0	3
4	0	1	4
5	1	2	0
⇒ 6	0	0	1
7	1	1	2
8	0	2	3
9	1	0	4
⇒ 10	0	1	0
11	1	2	1
12	0	0	2
13	1	1	3
14	0	2	4
⇒ 15	1	0	0
16	0	1	1
17	1	2	2
18	0	0	3
19	1	1	4
20	0	2	0
21	1	0	1
22	0	1	2
23	1	2	3
24	0	0	4
25	1	1	0
26	0	2	1
27	1	0	2
28	0	1	3
29	1	2	4

- 15 presses to get pattern 100

- 10 presses to get pattern 010

- 6 presses to get pattern 001

Me   "Now we just need to do some simple multiplication."

$$3 \times 5 = 15 \quad \rightarrow \text{pattern } 100$$

$$2 \quad \times 5 = 10 \quad \rightarrow \text{pattern } 010$$

$$2 \times 3 \quad = 6 \quad \rightarrow \text{pattern } 001$$

Yuri   "Where did that come from?"

Me   "Think about the situations when a clock comes all the way back to 0."

- The 2-clock returns to 0 on multiples of 2.

- The 3-clock returns to 0 on multiples of 3.

- The 5-clock returns to 0 on multiples of 5.

Yuri   "So?"

Me   "So for example, the 3-clock and the 5-clock will be on 0 when the number of button presses was both a multiple of 3 and a multiple of 5."

Yuri   "And that means you multiply?"

Me   "Right. Because if a number is a multiple of both 3 and 5, then it's a common multiple of those numbers. If both 3 and 5 are pointing at 0, then the pattern is something-00, where the 'something' is either 0 or 1."

Yuri   "Sure, okay."

Me   "Since $3 \times 5 = 15$, we know 15 is a common multiple of 3 and 5, and so 15 button presses will give a something-00 pattern. In fact it gives pattern 100, which is nice. Then you just keep thinking the same way."

- $3 \times 5 = 15$ presses gives pattern 100.

- $2 \times 5 = 10$ presses gives pattern 010.

- $2 \times 3 = 6$ presses gives pattern 001.

Yuri   "I'm with you so far. Keep going."

Me   "Well now we know how to make patterns 100, 010, and
            001, so we just have to think about groups of button
            presses."

- A group of 15 button presses advances just the 2-clock.

- A group of 10 button presses advances just the 3-clock.

- A group of 6 button presses advances just the 5-clock.

Yuri   "Yep, yep."

Me   "The rest is easy. You just advance the clocks one at a
            time until you get the pattern you're after."

Yuri   "Like setting a digital watch."

Me   "Something like that. First you set the hours, then the
            minutes, then the seconds. Let's try it for pattern 024."

- A group of 15 presses 0 times.

- A group of 10 presses 2 times.

- A group of 6 presses 4 times.

Yuri   "You just add those up?"

Me   "Right!"

$$15 \times \underline{0} + 10 \times \underline{2} + 6 \times \underline{4} = 0 + 20 + 24$$
$$= 44$$

Me   "Voilà, 44 presses gives pattern 024."

Yuri   "Hey, wait a sec. That's too many. The chart says we just need 14!"

Me   "And it also says that things stay the same after 30 presses. That means we can subtract 30s until we get the smallest positive number we can. In this case, $44 - 30 = 14$."

Yuri   "Oh, well, there ya go."

Me   "For bonus points, what's the name for the number you get after subtracting all the 30s you can without going negative?"

Yuri   "Er . . . Oh, I know! The remainder!"

Me   "Right. So instead of subtracting a bunch of times, you can divide by 30 and just look at the remainder. Here's a summary of everything we did."

How to solve the clock puzzle

We solved the puzzle with a 2-clock, a 3-clock, and a 5-clock as follows:

Step 1. We found the patterns that advance each clock individually by 1 (patterns 100, 010, and 001).

Step 2. We found the number of times to press the button to get each pattern (15, 10, and 6 times).

Step 3. We set each clock to its target value, one at a time (for pattern $\underline{0}2\underline{4}$, we press the button $15 \times \underline{0} + 10 \times \underline{2} + 6 \times \underline{4} = 44$ times).

Step 4. We divided the value we found in Step 3 by the least common multiple of the clock numbers (30), and took the remainder. This is the minimum number of times we need to press the button to get the target pattern ($44 \div 30 = 1$ with a remainder of 14).

Step 5. Adding this minimum number of button presses to multiples of the least common multiple ($30n$) gives a general term for the number of button presses resulting in the desired pattern ($30n + 14$, for $n = 0, 1, 2, 3, \dots$).

Yuri   "Okay, you win. Setting the clocks one at a time does the trick."

Me   "But it was your saying the problem would be easier with just one clock that gave me the hint."

Yuri   "Sometimes I'm unable to fully conceal my genius."

Me   "I wonder if we could—"

Yuri   "Hey, wait!"

Me   "What's wrong?"

Yuri   "I just realized that we did end up with just one clock after all!"

Me   "What do you mean?"

Yuri   "We divided by the least common multiple of 2, 3, and 5, right? And that said everything gets reset after 30 presses? Well isn't that sorta like working with one giant 30-clock?"

Me   "Huh...I guess it does. Something like this."

A 30-clock

Yuri   "Now *that's* a serious clock."

Mom   "Hey, kids! It's—"

Yuri   "Snack time!"

I kept thinking about this problem as we ate. Did we create a big 30-clock from the 2-, 3-, and 5-clocks? Or had we just been working with the parts of the 30-clock all along? A prime factorization of a 30-clock, as it were.

$$30 = 2 \times 3 \times 5$$

Since we could make patterns 100, 010, and 001, that meant we could make any pattern we wanted ... or did it? What would happen if the clock numbers weren't primes? If we could guarantee that we can create all the patterns like $(1, 0, \ldots, 0)$, then ...

So much math from such a simple toy.

"How can you say you did something if you can't show it?"

Problems for Chapter 4

Problem 4-1 (The clock puzzle)

For the clock puzzle described in this chapter, find a general term for the number of count button presses needed to generate the pattern 123 after the reset button has been pressed. (No peeking at the table on page 121!)

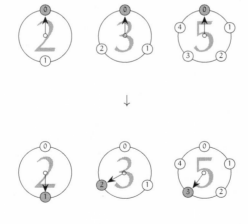

(Answer on page 199)

Problem 4-2 (The clock puzzle)

For the clock puzzle described in this chapter, find a general term for the number of count button presses needed to generate the pattern 124 after the reset button has been pressed. (No peeking at the table on page 121!)

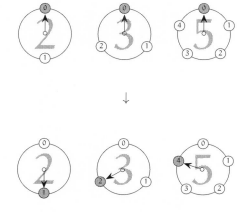

(Answer on page 200)

Problem 4-3 (The clock puzzle)

For the clock puzzle described in this chapter, find a general term for the number of count button presses needed to generate pattern 000 if you start from pattern 123. (No peeking at the table on page 121!)

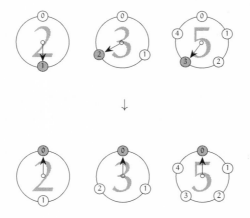

(Answer on page 201)

CHAPTER 5

Mathematical Induction

"You can start on any journey, so long
as you take that first step."

5.1 THE LIBRARY

I loved my school library. I always went there after school, usually
just to think. Sometimes I'd mess around with math, sometimes
I'd just stare into space and let my mind wander. The important
thing was that I didn't have to worry about the time. There were no
bells partitioning my time there, no sudden end to things like when
taking a test. Well, at least not until Ms. Mizutani would appear
and announce that the library was closed.

One day while I was reflecting on how much I enjoyed these quiet,
undisturbed moments, Tetra came moping in.

5.2 TETRA

Me   "Hey, Tetra. Looks like you've had better days."

Tetra   "I just heard that mathematical induction shows up on
our college entrance exams."

Me   "Sure."

Tetra   "That sounds...hard."

Me   "The name is intimidating, but it's not so bad. Don't let
             preconceived notions get in your way."

Tetra   "I don't suppose...Um..."

Me   "...that I'd help you learn it?"

Tetra   "Something like that, yeah."

Me   "No problem. Let's work through a problem together."

Tetra   "Thanks!"

We headed to the exam prep section of the library and looked for
math problems that called for induction. Flipping through a book of
questions from previous university entrance exams, I found a promis-
ing candidate.[1]

Me   "Looks like the second part of this problem calls for in-
             duction."

Tetra   "Let's give it a shot!"

Me   "Okay. The first step in solving any problem is to read
             it carefully."

---

[1]Credit: The problem discussed in this chapter is from the 2013 National
Center Test for University Admissions (Japan National Center for University
Entrance Examinations), Mathematics II-B exam, problem 3, part 2.

5.3 THE PROBLEM, PART I

Let $a_1 = 3, a_2 = 3, a_3 = 3$ be the first three terms in a sequence of positive numbers $\langle a_n \rangle$. Suppose that for all natural numbers n,

$$a_{n+3} = \frac{a_n + a_{n+1}}{a_{n+2}}. \qquad \textbf{Eq.} \; ②$$

Furthermore, let $\langle b_n \rangle$ and $\langle c_n \rangle$ be defined by $b_n = a_{2n-1}$ and $c_n = a_{2n}$. We wish to find the general terms for sequences $\langle b_n \rangle$ and $\langle c_n \rangle$.

First, from ② we have that

$$a_4 = \frac{a_1 + a_2}{a_3} = \boxed{L}, \, a_5 = 3, \, a_6 = \frac{\boxed{M}}{\boxed{N}}, \, a_7 = 3.$$

From this we obtain $b_1 = b_2 = b_3 = b_4 = 3$, so one might conjecture that

$$b_n = 3 \qquad (n = 1, 2, 3, \ldots). \qquad \textbf{Eq.} \; ③$$

We already know that $b_1 = 3$, so to demonstrate ③ it is sufficient to show that $b_{n+1} = b_n$ for all natural numbers n.

We can prove this by...

(continued in Part 2 on p. 160)

Tetra   "Whoa, whoa! Hold up, at least until my head stops spinning."

Me   "My bad. This is definitely a problem worth going through line-by-line."

Tetra   "You think? I've never even *seen* such a complicated problem, much less solved one."

Me   "When you're slammed with a problem like this on a test, it's easy to freeze up. It's important to learn to read problems like this quickly, but for now let's focus on being sure we understand it, one chunk at a time."

Tetra   "Divide and conquer."

Me   "Right. There's no point in moving ahead when you don't understand something, so let's take it piece by piece, and be sure we're following everything through to the end."

Tetra   "Agreed!"

5.4 SEQUENCES

Me   "So the problem starts out talking about a sequence of positive numbers $\langle a_n \rangle$."

Tetra   "I know what positive numbers are, at least! The ones with plusses, not minuses!"

Me   "Numbers greater than 0, right. And a sequence is just a bunch of numbers in some order. So $1, 2, 3, 4, \ldots$ is a sequence, and so is $0, 2, 4, 6, 8, \ldots$. You can even make a sequence like $-1, \frac{1}{2}, -\frac{1}{3}, \frac{1}{4}, -\frac{1}{5}, \ldots$."

Tetra   "But that one has negatives."

Me   "That one does, but the sequence in this problem won't. It says 'a sequence of positive numbers $\langle a_n \rangle$,' right? So there's a condition on this sequence, that it won't include 0 or any negative numbers."

Tetra   "Gotcha."

Me   "A general representation of a sequence looks something like this."

$$a_1, a_2, a_3, a_4, \ldots$$

Tetra   "And all the a's are really numbers, right?"

Me   "Sure, we just named them all using numbered a's. That orders them, too, so the first element in the sequence is a_1, the second is a_2, and so on. We've used subscripts like that before, right?"

Tetra   "We have."

Me   "Great. So this problem started out by naming a sequence $\langle a_n \rangle$, telling us what kind of sequence it is, and giving us the first few elements."

Let $a_1 = 3$, $a_2 = 3$, $a_3 = 3$ be the first three terms in a sequence of positive numbers $\langle a_n \rangle \ldots$

Tetra   "So the first number in the sequence is 3, and the second number is 3, and the third number is 3, too. So the whole sequence is all 3s?"

Me   "Not so fast. We only know that the first three elements are 3s. See? That's what I mean when I say not to have preconceived notions."

Tetra   "Oops! I'll be more careful."

Me   "Okay, so from reading carefully so far, we know that the sequence $\langle a_n \rangle$ starts out as $3, 3, 3$."

Tetra   "Right."

Me   "This problem has a lot of blanks to fill in—all these boxes with the letters in them—but we won't worry too much just yet. We have to approach this like we're solving the bigger problem first. If we can get a grip on the problem as a whole, the blanks will pretty much fill themselves in."

Tetra   "Looks like we've got some more reading to do, first."

5.5 Recursively Defining the Sequence

Me   "Let's read on, then. There's some more here about this
          sequence $\langle a_n \rangle$."

... a sequence of positive numbers $\langle a_n \rangle$ such that for all natural
numbers n

$$a_{n+3} = \frac{a_n + a_{n+1}}{a_{n+2}}. \qquad \textbf{Eq.}\ \textcircled{2}$$

Tetra   "Ugh. So many letters. And numbers on letters."

Me   "It's not a big deal. Just look at this equation labeled
           ② here, and tell me what you can get from it."

Tetra   "Like, that all the letters are a's with subscripts on
           them?"

Me   "Sure, that's important. And there are four of those—
           a_n, a_{n+1}, a_{n+2}, and a_{n+3}."

Tetra   "What does the n stand for?"

Me   "That's right here, where it says 'for all natural num-
           bers n.' A natural number is a number like $1, 2, 3, 4, \ldots$,
           so they're saying that this Equation ② is true for any of
           those numbers."

Tetra   "*They're* saying? Who are they?"

Me   "Whoever wrote the problem. That person is using
           Equation ② to define the sequence $\langle a_n \rangle$."

Tetra   "You can define sequences, too?"

Me   "You kinda have to. When the problem tells us $a_1 =
           3, a_2 = 3, a_3 = 3$ we can see the first three elements in
           the sequence, but nothing beyond that. But Equation
           ② describes $a_4, a_5, a_6, \ldots$, as far as you want to go."

Tetra   "Like, infinitely far?"

Me   "I guess you could say so, but that doesn't mean the definition never ends. It's more like, no matter how big a natural number n you want to use, a_n is there, defined for you. You want n to be 10000? No problem, just use Equation ② here."

Tetra   "Not to drag this out, but I'm still not clear on how we use Equation ②."

Me   "Let's look at it closely again. Pay attention to the form of the equation."

$$a_{n+3} = \frac{a_n + a_{n+1}}{a_{n+2}}. \qquad \textbf{Eq. ②}$$

Tetra   "It's … a fraction, I guess?"

Me   "That's good, but more important is that we have a_n, a_{n+1}, a_{n+2} on the right side, and a_{n+3} on the left."

Tetra   "How's that important?"

Me   "Because this means we can use Equation ② to calculate a_4 from a_1, a_2, a_3. That's gonna be *super* important."

Tetra   "We can calculate a_4 from a_1, a_2, a_3 …"

Me   "Try plugging 1 into the n's in ②."

Tetra   "Okay, then you get … ah! Sure enough, that's what it says."

Me   "Then when you replace the n's with 2?"

Tetra   "Oh, I get this now!"

- You can use a_1, a_2, a_3 to calculate a_4.

- You can use a_2, a_3, a_4 to calculate a_5.

- You can use a_3, a_4, a_5 to calculate $a_6 \ldots$

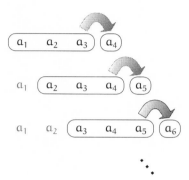

Me   "You've got it. So we can calculate a_n, for any natural
          number n, using two tools."

- The specific values $a_1 = 3, a_2 = 3, a_3 = 3$, and

- Equation ②

Me   "That's enough to define the sequence $\langle a_n \rangle$. That's why
          it's not so important just now that Equation ② is a frac-
          tion. What we're really after is how the sequence $\langle a_n \rangle$
          is defined."

Tetra   "A whole new way to look at equations!"

Me   "By the way, an equation like ② that defines a sequence
          is called a recurrence relation. So this problem is using
          a recurrence relation to define the sequence $\langle a_n \rangle$. So far
          so good?"

Tetra   "Surprisingly, yes!"

$$\begin{cases} a_1 & = 3 \\[4pt] a_2 & = 3 \\[4pt] a_3 & = 3 \\[4pt] a_{n+3} & = \dfrac{a_n + a_{n+1}}{a_{n+2}} \quad (n = 1, 2, 3, \ldots) \end{cases}$$

Defining $\langle a_n \rangle$ using a recursion formula

Me   "That's what happens when you read carefully enough—you understand things. Sorry we haven't gotten to mathematical induction yet, though."

Tetra   "No, this is great! I'm learning a lot already, and I can feel all this stuff getting sorted out in my head."

Me   "Glad to hear it. Okay, let's keep moving."

5.6 Calculating Terms

Tetra   "One other thing before we go any farther, if that's okay."

Me   "You name it."

Tetra   "Now that I understand how to use Equation ②, I'd kinda like to try calculating some terms in the sequence. Ones like a_4, a_5, a_6 that we don't know yet."

Me   "Actually, that's a great idea. Surprised I didn't think of it myself."

Tetra   "Cool! Okay, a_4 first."

$$a_{n+3} = \frac{a_n + a_{n+1}}{a_{n+2}} \qquad \text{Eq. ②}$$

$$a_{1+3} = \frac{a_1 + a_{1+1}}{a_{1+2}} \qquad \text{substitute } n = 1$$

$$a_4 = \frac{a_1 + a_2}{a_3} \qquad \text{calculate subscripts}$$

$$= \frac{3 + 3}{3} \qquad \text{use } a_1 = 3, a_2 = 3, a_3 = 3$$

$$= \frac{6}{3} \qquad \text{calculate } 3 + 3 = 6$$

$$= 2 \qquad \text{calculate } 6 \div 3 = 2$$

Me   "Great! So now we know that $a_4 = 2$."

Tetra   "Now for a_5!"

$$a_{n+3} = \frac{a_n + a_{n+1}}{a_{n+2}} \qquad \text{Eq. ②}$$

$$a_{2+3} = \frac{a_2 + a_{2+1}}{a_{2+2}} \qquad \text{substitute } n = 2$$

$$a_5 = \frac{a_2 + a_3}{a_4} \qquad \text{calculate subscripts}$$

$$= \frac{3 + 3}{2} \qquad \text{use } a_2 = 3, a_3 = 3, a_4 = 2$$

$$= \frac{6}{2} \qquad \text{calculate } 3 + 3 = 6$$

$$= 3 \qquad \text{calculate } 6 \div 2 = 3$$

Me   "So $a_5 = 3$. Hmm..."

Tetra   "Looks like it. Okay, a_6, here we come!"

$$a_{n+3} = \frac{a_n + a_{n+1}}{a_{n+2}} \qquad \text{Eq. } ②$$

$$a_{3+3} = \frac{a_3 + a_{3+1}}{a_{3+2}} \qquad \text{substitute } n = 3$$

$$a_6 = \frac{a_3 + a_4}{a_5} \qquad \text{calculate subscripts}$$

$$= \frac{3 + 2}{3} \qquad \text{use } a_3 = 3, a_4 = 2, a_5 = 3$$

$$= \frac{5}{3} \qquad \text{calculate } 3 + 2 = 5$$

Me   "And we get $a_6 = \frac{5}{3}$."

Tetra   "A fraction? Did I do something wrong?"

Me   "There's nothing wrong with fractions in a sequence."

Tetra   "If you say so. Let's do just one more!"

$$a_{n+3} = \frac{a_n + a_{n+1}}{a_{n+2}} \qquad \text{Eq. } ②$$

$$a_{4+3} = \frac{a_4 + a_{4+1}}{a_{4+2}} \qquad \text{substitute } n = 4$$

$$a_7 = \frac{a_4 + a_5}{a_6} \qquad \text{calculate subscripts}$$

$$= \frac{2 + 3}{\frac{5}{3}} \qquad \text{use } a_4 = 2, a_5 = 3, a_6 = \frac{5}{3}$$

$$= \frac{2 + 3}{\frac{5}{3}} \cdot \frac{\frac{3}{5}}{\frac{3}{5}} \qquad \text{get rid of fractional denominator}$$

$$= 5 \times \frac{3}{5} \qquad \text{denominators cancelled}$$

$$= 3 \qquad \text{calculate}$$

Me   "And so $a_7 = 3$."

Tetra   "Wow, it feels so much better to be back to natural number answers. Anyway, now we've got a_1 through a_7!"

n	1	2	3	4	5	6	7	...
a_n	3	3	3	2	3	$\frac{5}{3}$	3	...

Me   "Yeah, and look what—"

Tetra   "Don't stop me now, this is too much fun!"

Me   "You're missing something, though."

Tetra   "That there's infinitely many of these, so I've got to stop sometime? I know, but—"

Me   "It's not that. Look at the original problem, and see what you've done."

Tetra   "Uh, what did I do?"

Me   "You answered parts $\boxed{L}$, $\boxed{M}$, $\boxed{N}$ of the problem!"

Tetra   "I did?"

First, from ② we have that

$$a_4 = \frac{a_1 + a_2}{a_3} = \boxed{L}, \quad a_5 = 3, \quad a_6 = \frac{\boxed{M}}{\boxed{N}}, \quad a_7 = 3.$$

From this we...

Tetra   "I did! Let's see... $\boxed{L}$ is a_4, so that's 2. And $a_6 = \frac{5}{3}$, so $\boxed{M}$ is 5 and $\boxed{N}$ is 3! Neat!"

Me   "That's pretty insightful, seeing the recurrence relation and immediately wanting to calculate some actual values."

Tetra   "What can I say? I'm a natural."

5.7 DEFINING SEQUENCES WITH SEQUENCES

Me   "Back to the problem. There are a couple more sequences
          we need to use."

> Furthermore, define sequences $\langle b_n \rangle$, $\langle c_n \rangle$ such that for all natu-
> ral numbers n, $b_n = a_{2n-1}, c_n = a_{2n}$. We wish to find general
> terms for sequences $\langle b_n \rangle$, $\langle c_n \rangle$.

Tetra   "Oh, wow ... uh ... "

Me   "No need to panic. First off, what are the two new se-
          quences?"

Tetra   "One called $\langle b_n \rangle$ and one called $\langle c_n \rangle$."

Me   "Right. And do you see how each of those is defined?"

Tetra   "Umm ... sure. It even says 'define' right there in the
          problem, doesn't it. And it says to do it like this."

$$b_n = a_{2n-1} \qquad \text{definition of } \langle b_n \rangle$$
$$c_n = a_{2n} \qquad \text{definition of } \langle c_n \rangle$$

Me   "Perfect. So this means they're using $\langle a_n \rangle$ to define both
          $\langle b_n \rangle$ and $\langle c_n \rangle$, right?"

Tetra   "There's that 'they' again! It almost feels like *they* are
          setting up the rules to a game ... "

Me   "That's a pretty good analogy, actually. And here's one
          of the rules. How do you read this?"

$$b_n = a_{2n-1}$$

Tetra   "Um, that b_n equals a_{2n-1}? Is that wrong?"

Me   "No, it's not wrong, but let me give you another way.
          Since we're defining a sequence here, a good way to think
          of this is 'b_n is defined as a_{2n-1}.' So what's this a_{2n-1}
          that's defining b_n?"

Tetra   "I guess it's . . . uh . . . term number $2n - 1$ in $\langle a_n \rangle$?"

Me   "Yeah, that's right too, but I probably didn't phrase that
           well. How about this? If you have $n = 1, 2, 3, 4, \ldots$, what
           does $2n - 1$ represent?"

Tetra   "Hey, you taught me this! The *odd* numbers!"

Me   "Right! Because when $n = 1, 2, 3, 4, 5, \ldots$, we get $2n-1 =$
           $1, 3, 5, 7, 9, \ldots$. So in plain words, this says we create the
           sequence $\langle b_n \rangle$ by picking out the odd-numbered terms
           in sequence $\langle a_n \rangle$."

Tetra   "Ooh, and since $\langle c_n \rangle$ is a_{2n}, that one gets the even
           terms!"

Me   "Exactly!"

- $\langle b_n \rangle$ is the sequence $a_1, a_3, a_5, a_7, a_9, \ldots$

- $\langle c_n \rangle$ is the sequence $a_2, a_4, a_6, a_8, a_{10}, \ldots$

Me   "Let's read a little more of the problem. It's being nice,
           and telling us where all this is headed."

We wish to find general terms for sequences $\langle b_n \rangle, \langle c_n \rangle$.

Me   "What do you think the key words are here?"

Tetra   "General terms?"

Me   "Yep. You can write the general term for $\langle b_n \rangle$ as just
           b_n, and the general term for $\langle c_n \rangle$ as c_n."

Tetra   "So it's, like, the answer to 'What's the nth term in the
           sequence?' "

Me   "Exactly like that. The best answer to that question is
           a general term for the sequence, expressed using n."

Tetra   "Hang on a second ..."

Tetra begins scribbling in her notebook.

Tetra   " '... expressed using n.' Okay, got it."

Me   "So now we know that our goal is to find general terms for the sequences $\langle b_n \rangle, \langle c_n \rangle$. Next, the problem goes on and talks about the a_4, a_5, a_6, a_7 that you already found."

First, from ② we have that

$$a_4 = \frac{a_1 + a_2}{a_3} = \boxed{K}, a_5 = 3, a_6 = \frac{\boxed{L}}{\boxed{M}}, a_7 = 3.$$

Tetra   "Yep, and the answers should be 2 for $\boxed{K}$, 5 for $\boxed{L}$, and 3 for $\boxed{M}$."

Me   "This also lets us check your answers for a_5 and a_7. See here? It says 3 for both. Looks like you were right."

Tetra   "Wow, now I feel like I wasted my time calculating them, if they're going to show up in the problem like that."

Me   "Don't be silly. You should think of this as verifying that you're doing things right."

Tetra   "Good point! C'mon, let's read some more."

5.8 Guessing at the Sequence

From this we obtain $b_1 = b_2 = b_3 = b_4 = 3$, so one might conjecture that

$$b_n = 3 \qquad (n = 1, 2, 3, \ldots). \qquad \textbf{Eq.}\;③$$

Me   "Do you understand what the problem is saying here?"

Tetra   "I do!   It's saying that b_1, b_2, b_3, b_4 are the odd-numbered terms a_1, a_3, a_5, a_7, and those all equal 3. So b_5 and b_6 and all the other b's down the line probably equal 3, too!"

Me   "That's not quite the nuance. The 'one might conjecture' here implies that $b_n = 3$ is a good guess, but we can't be sure yet. After all, we only know for sure that the first four elements are 3. That doesn't tell us anything about b_5, or b_6, or b_{10000}."

Tetra   "Hmm, I guess you're right. So we have to calculate some more values?"

Me   "I don't think that's what we want to do here."

Tetra   "No? It helped before."

Me   "Yeah, but no matter how many values you calculate, you'll still have only checked what you've checked."

Tetra   "Well of course. How can you do better than that?"

Me   "By using the power of mathematics to create a proof."

5.9 Proof

Me   "Let's read a little more of the problem."

We already know that $b_1 = 3$, so to demonstrate ③ it is sufficient to show that $b_{n+1} = b_n$ for all natural numbers n.

| Me | "See how they're using the words 'show' and 'demonstrate' here? In mathematics, words like this often mean to *prove* something. So you could also read that sentence like this." |

...to **prove** ③ it is sufficient to **prove** that $b_{n+1} = b_n$ for all natural numbers n.

| Tetra | "Sorry to go off track here, but I have a question." |

| Me | "Ask away." |

| Tetra | "Where it says 'for all natural numbers n' here—that means 'for any n, which can be 1 or 2 or any other natural number,' right?" |

| Me | "That's right. We need to prove that $b_{n+1} = b_n$ when n is any natural number. This problem uses the phrase 'for all natural numbers n,' but you'll also see that worded '*any* natural number n,' or '*each* natural number n,' or '*every* natural number n,' or '*a given* natural number n.' They all mean the same thing." |

| Tetra | "Okay...But wording aside, how's that possible? I mean, there are infinitely many n's, right?" |

| Me | "There are indeed, and that's the beauty of problems like this. That's what makes them so hard, but also what makes them so interesting. And that's exactly why this problem needs a mathematical proof." |

| Tetra | "Mmm..." |

Me   "Don't worry. Once we get through the proof, you'll see
            why having infinitely many numbers to work with isn't
            a problem."

Tetra   "If you say so. Seems like you're going to have to use
            magic, though."

Me   "Mathematics has lots of ways for dealing with the infi-
            nite. And there's a particularly good method for dealing
            with the natural numbers."

Tetra   "That being?"

Me   "None other than...*mathematical induction*."

Tetra   "Ah! That's what I came here to ask you about!"

Me   "Let's read on. The problem is just about to get to that
            part."

5.10 THE PROBLEM, PART II

(Continued from Part 1, on p. 145)

...We can prove this by showing that ④ holds when $n = 1$, then
showing that if ④ holds when $n = k$, then ④ must also hold
when $n = k + 1$. Doing a mathematical proof in this manner is
called proof by ☐.

What is the most appropriate phrase to insert into ☐?

1. synthetic division   2. circular measure
3. mathematical induction   4. contradiction

(Continued in Part 3 on p. 168)

Tetra   "Uh..."

Me   "Well, I know you can guess what the answer for ☐
            is."

Tetra   "It's gotta be 3, mathematical induction. What do these other ones mean?"

Me   "Synthetic division is a way of dividing polynomials, and circular measure is about measuring angles using radians instead of degrees. So neither of those is even a method of proof. Contradiction here is a method of proof—where you assume that the thing you want to prove is false, then show how that leads to a contradiction—but that doesn't have anything to do with this proof."

Tetra stares at the page.

Me   "Something bothering you? If it's about proof by contradiction, I—"

Tetra   "No, I'm still just a bit overwhelmed by this problem. I can't make heads or tails of this part here."

We can prove this by showing that ④ holds when $n = 1$, then showing that if ④ holds when $n = k$, then ④ must also hold when $n = k + 1$.

Me   "Yeah, it's kind of a compact description, isn't it. Let me do some unpacking for you. Mathematical induction is easier to understand if you think of it happening in two steps."

The 2 steps of mathematical induction

Step A

     Prove that ④ is true when $n = 1$.

Step B

     Prove that if you assume ④ is true when $n = k$, then ④ is also true when $n = k + 1$

Tetra   "Well, now I can see the two steps at least."

Me   "And you can see that right now we're only interested in this Equation ④, right?"

$$b_{n+1} = b_n \qquad \textbf{Eq.} \ ④$$

Tetra   "Sure. This equation is all about sequence $\langle b_n \rangle$, I guess."

Me   "Right. Also keep our final goal in mind. We want to show that ④ is true for all natural numbers n. As you can see, n plays an important role in this equation."

Tetra   "What's it doing, exactly?"

Me   "When the value of n changes, ④ here says a different thing. Like, if $n = 1$, it says this."

$$b_2 = b_1 \qquad \text{Eq.} ④, \text{ when } n = 1$$

Tetra   "Yeah, I see that."

Me   "So what happens when $n = 2$?"

Tetra   "You get this."

$$b_3 = b_2 \qquad \text{Eq.} ④, \text{ when } n = 2$$

Me   "Right. What we want to prove is that ④ is true when $n = 1$, and when $n = 2$, and when $n = 3$, and when n is any other natural number."

Tetra   "That leads us back to having infinitely many natural numbers to prove."

Me   "Which seems like a problem because we can't keep showing that $b_2 = b_1$, and that $b_3 = b_2$, and so on until we're done."

Tetra   "Because we'd never get to 'done'!"

Tetra gives an emphatic nod.

Me   "That's where mathematical induction comes in. Let's take a closer look at it, starting with step A."

5.11 STEP A

The 2 steps of mathematical induction

Step A

Prove that ④ is true when $n = 1$.

Step B

Prove that if you assume ④ is true when $n = k$, then ④ is also true when $n = k + 1$

Me	"Step A says we need to prove that ④ is true when $n = 1$. What does that mean?"
Tetra	"I...uh...well..."
Me	"C'mon, spit it out."
Tetra	"Well, this is probably wrong, but does it mean we need to show that $b_2 = b_1$?"
Me	"That's *exactly* what it means."
Tetra	"Whew! That's a relief. But still, just showing this for $n = 1$? Seems like an awful lot of fuss over a simple little thing."

Tetra cocks an eyebrow.

Me	"Maybe so, but it's a necessary fuss if you're going to use mathematical induction."
Tetra	"I'll just take your word for now. What's next?"
Me	"Well, can you prove that $b_2 = b_1$?"
Tetra	"I don't think I can *prove* it, but earlier we found that $b_1 = 3$ and $b_2 = 3$, so I'm pretty sure that $b_2 = b_1$."

Me   "But Tetra, that's a proof."

Tetra   "Whoa, really? When I hear 'proof' I get this image of a
              whole bunch of difficult equations and stuff."

Me   "That's not always true. Just showing that b_2 and b_1
              are both 3 is a perfectly fine proof that $b_2 = b_1$."

Tetra   "Well whaddaya know."

Me   "And that's it for step A! Ready for step B?"

Tetra   "You bet!"

5.12 STEP B

Me   "Okay, let's look closely at step B. This is the heart of
              mathematical induction."

The 2 steps of mathematical induction

Step A

   Prove that ④ is true when $n = 1$.

Step B

   Prove that if you assume ④ is true when
   $n = k$, then ④ is also true when $n = k + 1$

Tetra   "It's also the one that makes me dizzy."

Me   "Not if we take it slow. There are just two important
              things to look at here, the k case and the $k + 1$ case."

Tetra   "Yeah, I see those on the page, but ..."

              Tetra grimaces, and my mind races.

Me   "How to explain... I know! It's like knocking over domi-
            noes!"

Tetra   "Like, when you knock one over and start a chain reac-
            tion?"

Me   "Exactly like that! Step A is like knocking over that first
            domino."

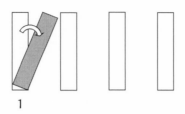

Step A, the first domino falls

Tetra   "Um...okay."

Me   "Then Step B is like saying, 'If domino number k gets
            knocked over, then domino k + 1 will get knocked over
            too.' "

**Step B, knocking over domino k will also knock over
domino k + 1**

Tetra   "So they're falling down, one after another."

Me   "That's right. And if step A and step B are both true,
            then the nth domino is going to fall, eventually, no mat-
            ter how big n is. Like, if n = 100, it goes like this."

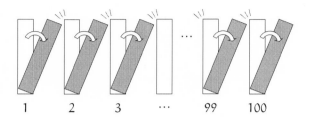

The 100th domino will eventually fall

Tetra   "Something like this?"

- The 1st domino falls
  (Step A)

- The 1st domino fell, so the 2nd domino will fall
  (Step B, when k = 1)

- The 2nd domino fell, so the 3rd domino will fall
  (Step B, when k = 2)

- The 3rd domino fell, so the 4th domino will fall
  (Step B, when k = 3)
  ⋮

- The 99th domino fell, so the 100th domino will fall
  (Step B, when k = 99)

- **We can say that the 100th domino will fall.**

Me   "Right! And this is exactly how mathematical induction
            works."

Tetra   "It works like dominoes...? Oh, oh! I see! It's a
            metaphor! Every domino is an Equation ④!"

Me   "Good!"

- $\textcircled{4}$ holds when $n = 1$
  (Step A)

- $\textcircled{4}$ holds when $n = 1$, so it holds when $n = 2$
  (Step B, when $k = 1$)

- $\textcircled{4}$ holds when $n = 2$, so it holds when $n = 3$
  (Step B, when $k = 2$)

- $\textcircled{4}$ holds when $n = 3$, so it holds when $n = 4$
  (Step B, when $k = 3$)
  $\vdots$

- $\textcircled{4}$ holds when $n = 99$, so it holds when $n = 100$
  (Step B, when $k = 99$)

- **We can say that $\textcircled{4}$ holds when $n = 100$.**

Tetra   "So proving step B—that if $\textcircled{4}$ is true when $n = k$ it's
            also true when $n = k + 1$—is like proving that all the
            dominoes will fall!"

Me   "Sounds like you've got it."

Tetra   "But there's no way I could have figured this out just by
            looking at a problem on a test. All those n's and k's
            flying around, makes it kinda hard to see the dominoes!"

Me   "That's why we practice first."

5.13 The Problem, Part III

Me   "Let's get back to the problem. It looks like what we
            called step A and step B are labelled (I) and (II) here."

(continued from Part 2 on p. 160)

(I) When $n = 1$, we have $b_1 = 3, b_2 = 3$, and so ④ holds.

(II) Suppose that ④ holds when $n = k$. In other words, suppose that

$$b_{k+1} = b_k. \qquad \textbf{Eq. ⑤}$$

Now consider the $n = k + 1$ case. If we substitute $2k$ for n in ② we obtain

$$b_{k+2} = \frac{c_k + \boxed{P}_{k+1}}{\boxed{Q}_{k+1}}.$$

Similarly, if we substitute $2k - 1$ for n in ② we obtain

$$c_{k+1} = \frac{\boxed{R}_k + c_k}{\boxed{S}_{k+1}}.$$

Therefore, b_{k+2} can be expressed as

$$b_{k+2} = \frac{(\boxed{T}_k + \boxed{U}_{k+1})\boxed{V}_{k+1}}{b_k + c_k}.$$

From ⑤ it thus follows that $b_{k+2} = b_{k+1}$, and so ④ also holds for $n = k + 1$.

From (I), (II) above, we have shown that ④ holds for all natural numbers n. Therefore ③ holds, and the general term for sequence $\langle b_n \rangle$ is $b_n = 3$. □

(End of problem)

Tetra   "Oh wow, another mess to trudge through."

Me	"I guess it looks that way at first, but just keep our two steps in mind. This part follows right along."
Tetra	"Okay, I'll be on the lookout for dominoes."
Me	"Then let's start by reading this carefully."

(I) When $n = 1$, we have $b_1 = 3, b_2 = 3$, and so ④ holds.

Me	"Line (I) here is equivalent to our step A. In other words—"
Tetra	"I've got this! They're knocking over the first domino, right?"
Me	"You're really into this domino thing, aren't you."

(II) Suppose that ④ holds when $n = k$. In other words, suppose that

$$b_{k+1} = b_k. \qquad \textbf{Eq. } ⑤$$

Me	"This part is the first half of step B. They're talking about when $n = k$, so this is describing when the kth domino falls."
Tetra	"But we haven't gotten to showing how it's going to knock down the next domino yet."
Me	"Not yet. The important thing here is that we're now free to use the equation $b_{k+1} = b_k$."
Tetra	"Use it how?"

Me   "As if $b_{k+1} = b_k$ is a true statement in the rest of the proof. Right now we're thinking about what happens to the next domino *if the kth domino falls*, right? That means we have to move ahead under the assumption that $b_{k+1} = b_k$ holds. We can expect this equation to show up at some key point in the proof."

Tetra   "I'll look forward to it!"

Now consider the $n = k + 1$ case. If we substitute $2k$ for n in ② we obtain

$$b_{k+2} = \frac{c_k + \boxed{P}_{k+1}}{\boxed{Q}_{k+1}}.$$

Similarly, if we substitute $2k - 1$ for n in ② we obtain

$$c_{k+1} = \frac{\boxed{R}_k + c_k}{\boxed{S}_{k+1}}.$$

Therefore . . .

Me   "Is this the part you think looks like a mess?"

Tetra   "That's a big chunk of it."

Me   "Actually, here the authors are taking our hand and guiding us to the solution. If we just follow their lead, we should be able to solve this."

Tetra   "Follow their lead? How?"

Me   "By just doing what the problem says. Let's substitute $2k$ for n in ②, like they suggest. Then we immediately get this."

$$a_{n+3} = \frac{a_n + a_{n+1}}{a_{n+2}} \qquad \text{Eq. ②}$$

$$\Downarrow$$

$$a_{2k+3} = \frac{a_{2k} + a_{2k+1}}{a_{2k+2}} \qquad \text{let } n = 2k, \text{ as suggested}$$

Tetra   "Sure, that's what we get ... but where on earth did that 2k come from?"

Me   "Good question. It looks like they're trying to use the sequences $\langle b_n \rangle$ and $\langle c_n \rangle$ to get somewhere."

Tetra   "Huh? But we just created an equation for sequence $\langle a_n \rangle$, right? Why did $\langle b_n \rangle$ show up?"

Me   "Well, b_n and c_n are defined as $b_n = a_{2n-1}, c_n = a_{2n}$, so it isn't hard to go back and forth."

Tetra   "Hang on just a sec."

             Tetra flips through her notes.

Tetra   "Oh, right. Sequence $\langle b_n \rangle$ is the odd terms from $\langle a_n \rangle$, and $\langle c_n \rangle$ is the even ones."

- Sequence $\langle b_n \rangle$ is $a_1, a_3, a_5, a_7, a_9, \ldots$

- Sequence $\langle c_n \rangle$ is $a_2, a_4, a_6, a_8, a_{10}, \ldots$

Me   "Like I said, let's just follow their lead, and see where they take us. Time to do some calculations."

5.14 FOLLOWING THEIR LEAD

Me   "Watch me work this out, and tell me if I make any dumb mistakes."

$$a_{n+3} = \frac{a_n + a_{n+1}}{a_{n+2}} \qquad \text{Eq. ②}$$

$$a_{\boxed{2k}+3} = \frac{a_{\boxed{2k}} + a_{\boxed{2k}+1}}{a_{\boxed{2k}+2}} \qquad \text{substitute } 2k \text{ for } n \text{ in ②}$$

$$a_{\boxed{2(k+2)-1}} = \frac{a_{2k} + a_{2k+1}}{a_{2k+2}} \qquad \begin{array}{l}\text{rewrite as} \\ 2k + 3 = 2(k+2) - 1\end{array}$$

$$\boxed{b_{k+2}} = \frac{a_{2k} + a_{2k+1}}{a_{2k+2}} \qquad \begin{array}{l}\text{(odd subscripts)} \\ \text{use } a_{2(k+2)-1} = b_{k+2}\end{array}$$

$$b_{k+2} = \frac{\boxed{c_k} + a_{2k+1}}{a_{2k+2}} \qquad \begin{array}{l}\text{(even subscripts)} \\ \text{use } a_{2k} = c_k\end{array}$$

$$b_{k+2} = \frac{c_k + a_{\boxed{2(k+1)-1}}}{a_{2k+2}} \qquad \begin{array}{l}\text{rewrite as} \\ 2k + 1 = 2(k+1) - 1\end{array}$$

$$b_{k+2} = \frac{c_k + \boxed{b_{k+1}}}{a_{2k+2}} \qquad \begin{array}{l}\text{(odd subscripts)} \\ \text{use } a_{2(k+1)-1} = b_{k+1}\end{array}$$

$$b_{k+2} = \frac{c_k + b_{k+1}}{a_{\boxed{2(k+1)}}} \qquad \text{rewrite as } 2k + 2 = 2(k+1)$$

$$b_{k+2} = \frac{c_k + b_{k+1}}{\boxed{c_{k+1}}} \qquad \begin{array}{l}\text{(even subscripts)} \\ \text{use } a_{2(k+1)} = c_{k+1}\end{array}$$

Tetra　　"Erk... What just happened?"

Me　　"I just created an a_{odd} form and converted that into sequence $\langle b_n \rangle$, then did the same with a_{even} and $\langle c_n \rangle$. In the end, I got this."

$$b_{k+2} = \frac{c_k + b_{k+1}}{c_{k+1}} \qquad \text{derived Eq. 1}$$

Tetra　　"But... but... there's no way I'd think to do something like this on a test!"

Me　　"You don't have to, the problem tells you to, right here. See? You have to put things in the form $b_{k+2} = \cdots$ to get answers $\boxed{P}$ and $\boxed{Q}$."

$$b_{k+2} = \frac{c_k + \boxed{P}_{k+1}}{\boxed{Q}_{k+1}} \qquad \text{from the problem}$$

Tetra   "Oh ... I guess you do, huh."

Me   "They've even gone so far as to give us the $k + 1$ subscripts on $\boxed{P}_{k+1}$ and $\boxed{Q}_{k+1}$. Now all we have to do is compare this with the equation I just derived."

Tetra   "So the answer for $\boxed{P}$ is b, and $\boxed{Q}$ is c?"

Me   "I sure hope so!"

5.15 ONE MORE TIME

Me   "Now we do something similar to calculate c_{k+1}. That should give us answers $\boxed{R}$ and $\boxed{S}$."

$$a_{n+3} = \frac{a_n + a_{n+1}}{a_{n+2}} \qquad \text{Eq. } \textcircled{2}$$

$$a_{\boxed{2k-1}+3} = \frac{a_{\boxed{2k-1}} + a_{\boxed{2k-1}+1}}{a_{\boxed{2k-1}+2}} \qquad \text{substitute } 2k - 1 \text{ for } n \text{ in } \textcircled{2}$$

$$a_{2k+2} = \frac{a_{2k-1} + a_{2k}}{a_{2k+1}} \qquad \text{calculate subscripts}$$

$$a_{\boxed{2(k+1)}} = \frac{a_{2k-1} + a_{2k}}{a_{\boxed{2(k+1)-1}}} \qquad \text{prep for replacing sequences}$$

$$\boxed{c_{k+1}} = \frac{a_{2k-1} + \boxed{c_k}}{a_{2(k+1)-1}} \qquad \begin{array}{l} \text{if subscript is even,} \\ \text{replace with } \langle c_n \rangle \end{array}$$

$$c_{k+1} = \frac{\boxed{b_k} + c_k}{\boxed{b_{k+1}}} \qquad \begin{array}{l} \text{if subscript is odd,} \\ \text{replace with } \langle b_n \rangle \end{array}$$

Tetra   "That does look similar. So the equation you derived is this?"

$$c_{k+1} = \frac{b_k + c_k}{b_{k+1}} \qquad \text{derived Eq. } \mathbf{2}$$

Me   "Yep! So now we just compare that with what's in the problem."

$$c_{k+1} = \frac{\boxed{R}_k + c_k}{\boxed{S}_{k+1}} \qquad \text{from the problem}$$

Tetra   "So $\boxed{R}$ is b, and $\boxed{S}$ is b too!"

Me   "See? The problem led us straight to the answer."

Tetra   "I suppose it did..."

5.16 SECOND HALF

Me   "There's just a little bit more calculation to do."

Therefore, b_{k+2} can be expressed as

$$b_{k+2} = \frac{\left(\boxed{T}_k + \boxed{U}_{k+1}\right)\boxed{V}_{k+1}}{b_k + c_k}.$$

Me   "This is the second half of step B. We're on our way to showing that $b_{k+2} = b_{k+1}$."

Tetra   "Still looks like a mess, though."

Me   "I think we'll be okay. The problem is still pointing the way, and using the two equations we found should give us b_{k+2} without too much fuss."

$$\begin{cases} b_{k+2} = \dfrac{c_k + b_{k+1}}{c_{k+1}} & \text{derived Eq. } \mathbf{1} \\[3mm] c_{k+1} = \dfrac{b_k + c_k}{b_{k+1}} & \text{derived Eq. } \mathbf{2} \end{cases}$$

Tetra   "If you say so."

Me   "No, really. We just need to set these up as a system of simultaneous equations and get rid of the c_{k+1}. We can do that by replacing c_{k+1} in the denominator of Equation 1 with Equation 2."

$$b_{k+2} = \frac{c_k + b_{k+1}}{c_{k+1}} \qquad \text{derived Eq. } \mathbf{1}$$

$$= (c_k + b_{k+1}) \cdot \frac{1}{c_{k+1}} \qquad \text{pull it apart}$$

$$= (c_k + b_{k+1}) \cdot \frac{b_{k+1}}{b_k + c_k} \qquad \text{substitute reciprocal of derived Eq. } \mathbf{2}$$

$$= \frac{(c_k + b_{k+1})b_{k+1}}{b_k + c_k} \qquad \text{clean up}$$

Tetra   "So we end up with this?"

$$b_{k+2} = \frac{(c_k + b_{k+1})b_{k+1}}{b_k + c_k} \qquad \text{derived Eq. } \mathbf{3}$$

Me   "Yep. Now we just compare that with the problem."

$$b_{k+2} = \frac{\left(\boxed{T}_k + \boxed{U}_{k+1}\right)\boxed{V}_{k+1}}{b_k + c_k} \qquad \text{from the problem}$$

Tetra   "Which give us...c for $\boxed{T}$, b for $\boxed{U}$, and b for $\boxed{V}$!"

Me   "Now all we've gotta do is finish the proof."

Tetra   "There's *more*?"

Me   "Just a bit! Hang in there!"

5.17 Finishing the Proof

From ⑤ it thus follows that $b_{k+2} = b_{k+1}$, and so ④ also holds for $n = k + 1$.

Tetra   "Uh, ⑤ was ... let's see ... "

Me   "It's the kth domino! Remember that equation I said would show up at some key point?"

Tetra   "Looks like you were right!"

$$b_{k+1} = b_k \qquad \textbf{Eq. ⑤}$$

Me   "We can use ⑤ to erase the b_k from our Equation 3. Doing that completes the proof!"

$$
\begin{aligned}
b_{k+2} &= \frac{(c_k + b_{k+1})b_{k+1}}{b_k + c_k} && \text{derived Eq. 3}\\
&= \frac{(c_k + b_{k+1})b_{k+1}}{b_{k+1} + c_k} && \text{used ⑤ } b_{k+1} = b_k\\
&= \frac{(b_{k+1} + c_k)b_{k+1}}{b_{k+1} + c_k} && \text{cleaned up}\\
&= \frac{\cancel{(b_{k+1} + c_k)}b_{k+1}}{\cancel{b_{k+1} + c_k}} && \text{cancel}\\
b_{k+2} &= b_{k+1} && \text{derived equation}
\end{aligned}
$$

Tetra   "Wow, that cleaned up nice, didn't it."

Me   "Yeah, most of it cancels, because $b_{k+1} + c_k \neq 0$."

Tetra   "And good riddance!"

Me   "So that's it! We've proven that if the kth domino falls, then the $k + 1$ domino will fall too. And we know that because we proved that if $b_{k+1} = b_k$ then $b_{k+2} = b_{k+1}$, which was our step B, (II) in the problem."

Tetra   "Whew!"

Me   "This last bit is the finishing touch on a proof by mathematical induction."

From (I), (II) above, we have shown that ④ holds for all natural numbers n. Therefore ③ holds, and the general term for sequence $\langle b_n \rangle$ is $b_n = 3$.

5.18 Looking Back

Me   "Some of the calculation was a bit of work, but it's doable if you pay attention to where the problem is pointing."

Tetra   "It still feels a tad over my head, but I think if I go through all this with the dominoes in mind, I can understand it all. But . . ."

Me   "Something still bugging you?"

Tetra   "You did a great job showing me exactly how to solve the problem, but I still feel like we skirted around the whole issue, somehow."

Me   "Skirted around what?"

Tetra   "Well, the thing that gets me is how we can prove something about the natural numbers, despite there being infinitely many of them. When you compared it to dominoes I was like 'Oh, yeah! I get it!' But now I'm not so sure."

Me   "Er, well then, let's—"

Miruka   "What's this about dominoes?"

Tetra   "Hey, Miruka!"

We give Miruka a rundown of Tetra's concerns.

Miruka	"Hmph. Sounds like you're hung up on the idea of a finite proof of the infinite."
Tetra	"Maybe so. It's definitely the 'infinite' that's bothering me."
Me	"Considering the infinite can be tricky, I'll give you that."
Tetra	"Super tricky."
Miruka	"Well you're in good company. Dealing with the infinite has always been a major concern in mathematics. Did you notice that a proof by mathematical induction never directly mentions infinity?"
Me	"Hey, you're right. You just say something like 'for all natural numbers n.' "
Miruka	"That's because 'infinity' is a slippery word, so you can't directly apply it to a proof like this. Induction very carefully avoids the pitfalls you can fall into if you're careless. It's a beautiful example of the power of logic."
Tetra	"The power of logic . . . Wow."
Me	"And it defies infinity in just two steps. Pretty impressive."
Miruka	"Indeed. Induction is fundamentally important in proofs related to natural numbers."
Tetra	"It's that big a deal?"
Miruka	"The biggest of deals. Induction *defines* the natural numbers, in the Peano axioms."
Tetra	"What are the—"
Ms. Mizutani	"The library is *closed!*"

We had to leave the Peano axioms for another day. I was satisfied, though. Explaining the problem to Tetra had helped me solidify my own understanding of mathematical induction, viewed as both a two-step mathematical process and as toppling dominoes. I walked home, feeling newly empowered to take on the infinite.

"You can keep on going, so long as you take that next step."

Problems for Chapter 5

Problem 5-1 (Recurrence relations)

Define sequence $\langle F_n \rangle$ by the following recurrence relation:

$$\begin{cases} F_1 & = 1 \\ F_2 & = 1 \\ F_n & = F_{n-1} + F_{n-2} \qquad (n = 3, 4, 5, \ldots) \end{cases}$$

Find the first ten elements of $\langle F_n \rangle$ ($F_1, F_2, F_3, \ldots, F_{10}$).

(Answer on page 203)

Problem 5-2 (General terms)

Say that the first ten elements of sequence $\langle a_n \rangle$ are those listed in the table below:

n	1	2	3	4	5	6	7	8	9	10	$\cdots$
a_n	-1	3	-5	7	-9	11	-13	15	-17	19	$\cdots$

Determine a general term a_n for this sequence, represented in terms of n.

(Answer on page 204)

Problem 5-3 (Mathematical induction)

Use mathematical induction to prove that

$$1 + 2 + 3 + \cdots + n = \frac{n(n+1)}{2}$$

for a given positive integer n.

(Answer on page 205)

Problem 5-4 (Mathematical induction)

For the sequence $\langle F_n \rangle$ in Problem 5-1, use mathematical induction to prove that

$$F_1 + F_2 + F_3 + \cdots + F_n = F_{n+2} - 1$$

for a given positive integer n.

(Answer on page 206)

Epilogue

One day, in a quiet math department storeroom . . .

Girl   "Whoa, there's so much cool stuff in here!"

Teacher   "Yeah, it's fun to poke around."

Girl   "What's this?"

The girl picks up an old handout.

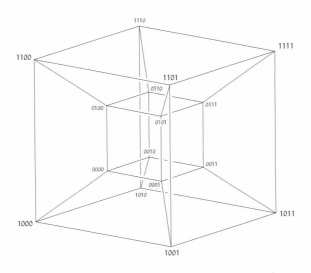

Teacher   "What do you think it is?"

Girl   "Some kind of solid?"

Teacher   "It is, but a four-dimensional one. A hypersolid."

Girl   "A *hyper*solid?"

Teacher   "Yeah, though this one is distorted because it's been crammed into three dimensions. See how the vertices are labelled?"

Girl   "Is that binary?"

Teacher   "You can look at it that way. You can also think of those as four-dimensional coordinates, like $(1, 0, 0, 1)$, with each component representing one of the binary bits. Vertices connected by edges have a bit flipped, and as you traverse the edges, one coordinate changes. It's all very regular."

Girl   "So there are 2^4 vertices, right?"

Teacher   "A perfect fit for 4 bits."

          The girl picks up another handout.

Girl   "What about this?"

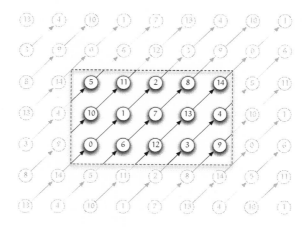

Teacher   "What do you think?"

Girl   "Diagonal sequences? With a bunch of lines?"

Teacher   "Actually that's just one line."

Girl   "Huh?"

Teacher   "Look at the 3 × 5 block in the middle. See the spiral?"

Girl   "So you follow this around in order?"

Teacher   "Right. If you look close, you'll find a doughnut."

Girl   "I'm ... not seeing that."

Teacher   "Try mentally connecting the upper and lower sides, so
              that the arrows match up, then bending the resulting
              tube around to join the right and left sides."

Girl   "Wow, it *is* a doughnut!"

Teacher   "Technically it's called a torus. So the diagram shows 15
              points on a line that's spiraling around the surface of a
              two-dimensional torus."

Girl   "And this?"

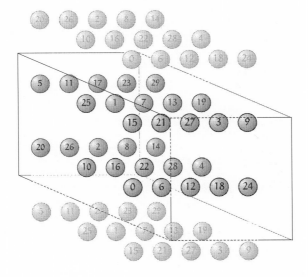

Teacher   "You tell me."

Girl   "Well ..."

Teacher   "Give up?"

Girl   "Hang on, still thinking. Let's see. If I follow the numbers in order ..."

Teacher   "Then ... ?"

Girl   "Got it! It's a *three*-dimensional torus! Same idea, but you've connected the top–bottom, left–right, and front–back surfaces. So this is $2 \times 3 \times 5 = 30$ points on the surface of a three-dimensional torus, connected by a single spiraling line!"

Teacher   "Well done."

Girl   "Nah, you're easy to read. You try to pull this one-more-dimension thing all the time."

Teacher   "Well then I'm glad to see you're finding patterns in repetition. There are patterns hidden everywhere, just waiting for you to find them and ride them to infinity."

Girl   "Sounds like a long ride."

Teacher   "Speaking of which, this 3D torus is also a clock puzzle."

Girl   "What kind of clock puzzle?"

Teacher   "One with dials with 2, 3, and 5 numbers on them."

Girl   "Because they're primes, I suppose?"

Teacher   "Exactly. The problem relies on 1 being the greatest common factor between any pair of the numbers."

Girl   "I'm gonna read you again, and bet that it takes $2 \times 3 \times 5 = 30$ ticks to work your way around that clock."

The girl laughs, waves, and spins away.

Answers to Problems

Problem 1-1 (Checking for multiples of 3)

Which of (a), (b), and (c) are multiples of 3?

(a) 123456

(b) 199991

(c) 111111

Answer 1-1 (Checking for multiples of 3)

We can answer this using the method described on p. 4.

(a) $1 + 2 + 3 + 4 + 5 + 6 = 21$, and 21 is evenly divided by 3, so 123456 must be a multiple of 3 too. (When you added the digits in this number, did you think to use paired 7s?)

(b) $1 + 9 + 9 + 9 + 9 + 1 = 38$, and 38 isn't evenly divided by 3, so 199991 can't be a multiple of 3.

(c) $1 + 1 + 1 + 1 + 1 + 1 = 6$, and 6 is evenly divided by 3, so 111111 must be a multiple of 3 too.

Answer: (a) and (c) are multiples of 3; (b) is not.

Incidentally, as discussed in Chapter 1, you don't have to add digits that are themselves multiples of 3. So in (a) you can ignore the 3 and the 6, and add just $1 + 2 + 4 + 5$. Taking that a step further, $1 + 2$ gives you 3, so you can ignore that bit. That leaves you with just $4 + 5 = 9$, which is easily identifiable as a multiple of 3.

In (b) you don't have to add the 9s, leaving you with just $1 + 1 = 2$, which is clearly not a multiple of 3.

In (c), all the digits are 1s. In numbers like that, you need only count the digits in the number, and see if that count is a multiple of 3.

$$1, 11, \underbrace{111}_{3\text{ digits}}, 1111, 11111, \underbrace{111111}_{6\text{ digits}}, 1111111, \cdots$$

Problem 1-2 (Representation as mathematical statements)

Let n be an **even** integer in the range $0 \leqslant n < 1000$. Letting a, b, c respectively be the hundreds, tens, and ones digits of n, what values can a, b, c take?

Answer 1-2 (Representation as mathematical statements)

The hundreds and tens digits can be any of $0, 1, 2, 3, \ldots, 9$. The problem states that n must be even, however, which means that the ones digit must be even. (If the ones digit is odd, then the number itself is odd too.)

Variables a, b, c can therefore take the following values:

$$a = 0, 1, 2, 3, 4, 5, 6, 7, 8, 9$$
$$b = 0, 1, 2, 3, 4, 5, 6, 7, 8, 9$$
$$c = 0, 2, 4, 6, 8$$

Problem 1-3 (Building a table)

In this chapter, the narrator used A_n to represent the sum of the digits in an integer n. For example, when $n = 316$,

$$A_{316} = 3 + 1 + 6 = 10.$$

Using that, fill in the blanks in the following table:

n	0	1	2	3	4	5	6	7	8	9
A_n										

n	10	11	12	13	14	15	16	17	18	19
A_n										

n	20	21	22	23	24	25	26	27	28	29
A_n										

n	30	31	32	33	34	35	36	37	38	39
A_n										

n	40	41	42	43	44	45	46	47	48	49
A_n										

n	50	51	52	53	54	55	56	57	58	59
A_n										

n	60	61	62	63	64	65	66	67	68	69
A_n										

n	70	71	72	73	74	75	76	77	78	79
A_n										

n	80	81	82	83	84	85	86	87	88	89
A_n										

n	90	91	92	93	94	95	96	97	98	99
A_n										

n	100	101	102	103	104	105	106	107	108	109
A_n										

Answer 1-3 (Building a table)

The completed table is as follows:

n	0	1	2	3	4	5	6	7	8	9
A_n	0	1	2	3	4	5	6	7	8	9

n	10	11	12	13	14	15	16	17	18	19
A_n	1	2	3	4	5	6	7	8	9	10

n	20	21	22	23	24	25	26	27	28	29
A_n	2	3	4	5	6	7	8	9	10	11

n	30	31	32	33	34	35	36	37	38	39
A_n	3	4	5	6	7	8	9	10	11	12

n	40	41	42	43	44	45	46	47	48	49
A_n	4	5	6	7	8	9	10	11	12	13

n	50	51	52	53	54	55	56	57	58	59
A_n	5	6	7	8	9	10	11	12	13	14

n	60	61	62	63	64	65	66	67	68	69
A_n	6	7	8	9	10	11	12	13	14	15

n	70	71	72	73	74	75	76	77	78	79
A_n	7	8	9	10	11	12	13	14	15	16

n	80	81	82	83	84	85	86	87	88	89
A_n	8	9	10	11	12	13	14	15	16	17

n	90	91	92	93	94	95	96	97	98	99
A_n	9	10	11	12	13	14	15	16	17	18

n	100	101	102	103	104	105	106	107	108	109
A_n	1	2	3	4	5	6	7	8	9	10

ANSWERS TO CHAPTER 2 PROBLEMS

Problem 2-1 (Primes)

Which of the following statements are mathematically accurate?

- (a) 91 is a prime number.

- (b) The sum of two primes is an even number.

- (c) If an integer 2 or greater is not a composite number, then it is a prime number.

- (d) All primes have exactly two factors.

- (e) All composite numbers have three or more factors.

Answer 2-1 (Primes)

(a) 91 is a prime number.

   This is false because $91 = 7 \times 13$, making it a composite number.

(b) The sum of two primes is an even number.

   This is false. For example, 2 and 3 are prime numbers, but $2 + 3 = 5$, and 5 is not an even number.

(c) If an integer 2 or greater is not a composite number, then it is a prime number.

   This is true. All integers 2 or greater are either prime or composite numbers.

(d) All primes have exactly two factors.

   This is true. A prime p has only two factors: itself and 1.

(e) All composite numbers have three or more factors.

> This is true. If an integer N is a composite number, it can be written as a product of two integers N = mn, where $1 < m < N$ and $1 < n < N$. This means that N must have at least three factors, N, 1, and m. Note that it's possible that $m = n$, so a composite number won't necessarily have four factors. For example, 9 is a composite number that can be written as $9 = 3 \times 3$, and 1, 3, and 9 are its only factors.

<u>Answer: (c), (d), and (e)</u>

Problem 2-2 (The Sieve of Eratosthenes)

Use the Sieve of Eratosthenes to find all prime numbers less than 200.

Answer 2-2 (The Sieve of Eratosthenes)

The result is something like this:

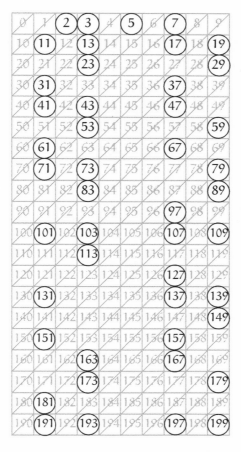

Table of primes less than 200

Problem 2-3 (Improving the Sieve of Eratosthenes)

The algorithm for the Sieve of Eratosthenes on p. 41 doesn't account for the fact that you can quit once $p^2 > N$. Improve the algorithm so that it takes advantage of this.

Answer 2-3 (Improving the Sieve of Eratosthenes)

For example, we can add the following Step 2':

Finding Primes Using the Sieve of Eratosthenes

You can find all primes less than a natural number N by the following algorithm:

Step 1. Create a table of numbers from 0 to N, and cross out zero (0) and the unit (1).

Step 2. If any numbers are left, circle the smallest remaining number, p. If no numbers are left, stop. (The circled number p is a prime number.)

Step 2'. If $p^2 > N$, circle all remaining numbers (each of them is prime), and stop.

Step 3. Cross out all multiples of prime p larger than p, and repeat **Step 2**. (The numbers you crossed out have p as a factor.)

When you're done, all primes in the table will be circled, and zero, the unit, and all composite numbers will be crossed out.

Problem 2-4 (The binomial $n^2 + n + 41$)

Prove that the binomial $P(n) = n^2 + n + 41$ results in an odd number for all integer values of $n \geqslant 0$.

Answer 2-4 (The binomial $n^2 + n + 41$)

Proof 1 (Separate cases)

We separately address the cases where n is even and odd.

If n **is even**, then n^2 is even too. Since 41 is odd, the form of $n^2 + n + 41$ is even + even + odd = odd.

If n **is odd**, then n^2 is odd too. Since 41 is odd, the form of $n^2 + n + 41$ is odd + odd + odd = odd.

It therefore follows that $P(n)$ returns only odd values.   □

Proof 2 (Equation manipulation)

Rewrite the equation as

$$n^2 + n + 41 = n(n + 1) + 41.$$

Here, one of either n or $n + 1$ must be even, so $n(n + 1)$ is even. $n(n + 1) + 41$ is thus the sum of an even and an odd number, which must be odd.

It therefore follows that $P(n)$ returns only odd values.   □

Problem 3-1 (Representing numbers with cards)

If you used Yuri's five cards to represent the number 25, what numbers would be in the upper-left corners?

Answer 3-1 (Representing numbers with cards)

You can use the method of repeated division described on p. 87 to find the answer:

$$25 \div 16 = 1 \text{ remainder } 9$$
$$9 \div 8 = 1 \text{ remainder } 1$$
$$1 \div 4 = 0 \text{ remainder } 1$$
$$1 \div 2 = 0 \text{ remainder } 1$$
$$1 \div 1 = 1 \text{ remainder } 0$$

We got a quotient of 1 when dividing by 16, 8, or 1, and we can confirm that $16 + 8 + 1 = 25$. Those are therefore the numbers that should appear in the upper-left corners of the cards.

Answer: $16, 8, 1$

Problem 3-2 (Numbers on the cards)

What other numbers would be on the card with a 2 in its upper-left corner? (No peeking at the appendix, please!)

```
2  ?  ?  ?
?  ?  ?  ?
?  ?  ?  ?
?  ?  ?  ?
```

Answer 3-2 (Numbers on the cards)

The card should look like this:

```
2  3  6  7
10 11 14 15
18 19 22 23
26 27 30 31
```

You can find these numbers in the range 0 to 31 by following the pattern "skip two, choose two." Another way to think of this is selecting those numbers that leave remainder 2 or 3 when divided by 4. In terms of the alligators discussed on p. 90, the numbers on the "2 card" are those that the alligator with the 2-sized mouth would get a bite of.

Answer: $2, 3, 6, 7, 10, 11, 14, 15, 18, 19, 22, 23, 26, 27, 30, 31$

Problem 3-3 (Multiples of 4)

Using Yuri's five cards, think of a way to know at a glance if someone is thinking of a number that's a multiple of 4. Be sure to arrange the cards so that the numbers in the upper-left corner are $16, 8, 4, 2, 1$, in that order.

Answer 3-3 (Multiples of 4)

A multiple of 4 is a number that leaves remainder 0 when divided by 4. In terms of the alligators discussed on p. 90, a multiple of 4 is a number that doesn't leave anything for the 2 or the 1 alligators to eat. That means cards to the right of the 4 card (the 2 and the 1 card) will be turned down if you're trying to find a multiple of 4.

Answer: If the two rightmost cards are turned down

Problem 3-4 (Flipping cards)

Suppose you've used Yuri's cards to represent some number N. What number would you get if you flipped every card, so that face-up cards became face down, and face-down cards became face-up? Give your answer using N.

Answer 3-4 (Flipping cards)

Note that if you flip a set of cards over, you're changing, for example, 11010 into 00101. When you add these two numbers together, you get 11111, which is 31 in base 2. Since N plus the 'flip' of N always adds up to 31, the flip is $31 - N$.

Answer: $31 - N$

Problem 3-5 (n cards)

Each of Yuri's five cards has sixteen numbers on them. If she instead had n cards, how many numbers would be on each?

Answer 3-5 (n cards)

When using n cards, you can create 2^n patterns representing numbers 0 to $2^n - 1$. Each card will be face up in one half of the possible patterns, so there will be 2^{n-1} (one half of 2^n) numbers on each card.

Answer: 2^{n-1} numbers

ANSWERS TO CHAPTER 4 PROBLEMS

Problem 4-1 (The clock puzzle)

For the clock puzzle described in this chapter, find a general term for the number of count button presses needed to generate the pattern 123 after the reset button has been pressed. (No peeking at the table on page 121!)

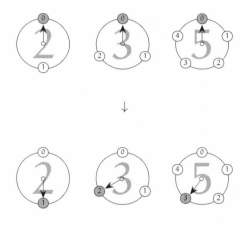

Answer 4-1 (The clock puzzle)

You can solve this using Step 3 and below of the puzzle solution method presented on p. 135.

Start by setting the clocks one at a time to the desired pattern 123.

$$15 \times \underline{1} + 10 \times \underline{2} + 6 \times \underline{3} = 15 + 20 + 18$$
$$= 53$$

Next, divide that number by the least common multiple of the numbers of the clocks (30), and take the remainder.

$$53 \div 30 = 1 \text{ remainder } 23$$

This means you need to push the count button at least 23 times. Put generally, you need to press the button

$$30n + 23 \qquad (n = 0, 1, 2, 3, \ldots)$$

times to get pattern 123.

Answer: $30n + 23 \qquad (n = 0, 1, 2, 3, \ldots)$

Problem 4-2 (The clock puzzle)

For the clock puzzle described in this chapter, find a general term for the number of count button presses needed to generate the pattern 124 after the reset button has been pressed. (No peeking at the table on page 121!)

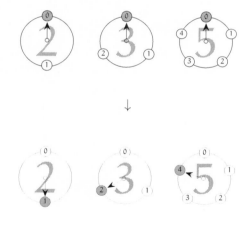

Answer 4-2 (The clock puzzle)

You can solve this in the same way as Problem 4-1, but you can also use the solution to that problem as a starting point.

Starting from the 123 pattern of Problem 4-1, to get the 124 pattern we need to move just the 5-clock's hand forward by one. As discussed in the chapter, pressing the count button 6 times has that effect.

$$([\text{number of presses to get pattern } 123] + 6) \div 30 = (23 + 6) \div 30$$
$$= 0 \text{ remainder } 29$$

Answer: $30n + 29$ $(n = 0, 1, 2, 3, \ldots)$

Alternate solution

One press from the 124 pattern gives the 000 pattern. From what we found before, that means we want one less than 30 button presses.

Answer: $30n + 29$ $(n = 0, 1, 2, 3, \ldots)$

Problem 4-3 (The clock puzzle)

For the clock puzzle described in this chapter, find a general term for the number of count button presses needed to generate pattern 000 if you start from pattern 123. (No peeking at the table on page 121!)

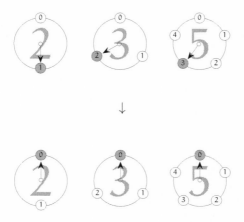

Answer 4-3 (The clock puzzle)

We found in Problem 4-1 that we need to press the button 23 times to create the 123 pattern. If you start with the 000 pattern and press the button 30 times, you wind up back at the 000 pattern, so to create the 000 pattern from the 123 pattern you need to press the button $30 - 23 = 7$ times.

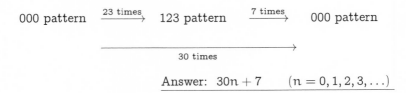

$$\text{Answer:} \quad 30n + 7 \qquad (n = 0, 1, 2, 3, \ldots)$$

ANSWERS TO CHAPTER 5 PROBLEMS

Problem 5-1 (Recurrence relations)

Define sequence $\langle F_n \rangle$ by the following recurrence relation:

$$\begin{cases} F_1 & = 1 \\ F_2 & = 1 \\ F_n & = F_{n-1} + F_{n-2} \quad (n = 3, 4, 5, \ldots) \end{cases}$$

Find the first ten elements of $\langle F_n \rangle$ ($F_1, F_2, F_3, \ldots, F_{10}$).

Answer 5-1 (Recurrence relations)

The first two terms are given as $F_1 = 1, F_2 = 1$. We use the recurrence relation to find F_3 and beyond.

$$\begin{aligned} F_3 &= F_2 + F_1 && \text{from the recurrence relation} \\ &= 1 + 1 && \text{from } F_2 = 1, F_1 = 1 \\ &= 2 \end{aligned}$$

Continuing with the recurrence relation,

$$\begin{aligned} F_4 &= F_3 + F_2 = 2 + 1 = 3 \\ F_5 &= F_4 + F_3 = 3 + 2 = 5 \\ F_6 &= F_5 + F_4 = 5 + 3 = 8 \\ F_7 &= F_6 + F_5 = 8 + 5 = 13 \\ F_8 &= F_7 + F_6 = 13 + 8 = 21 \\ F_9 &= F_8 + F_7 = 21 + 13 = 34 \\ F_{10} &= F_9 + F_8 = 34 + 21 = 55. \end{aligned}$$

The following summarizes the results:

n	1	2	3	4	5	6	7	8	9	10
F_n	1	1	2	3	5	8	13	21	34	55

Incidentally, this sequence has a name: the Fibonacci sequence.

Answer: $1, 1, 2, 3, 5, 8, 13, 21, 34, 55$

Problem 5-2 (General terms)

Say that the first ten elements of sequence $\langle a_n \rangle$ are those listed in the table below:

n	1	2	3	4	5	6	7	8	9	10	$\cdots$
a_n	-1	3	-5	7	-9	11	-13	15	-17	19	$\cdots$

Determine a general term a_n for this sequence, represented in terms of n.

Answer 5-2 (General terms)

Note that if their signs are ignored, the terms in $\langle a_n \rangle$ are the odd natural numbers. Also note that when n is odd, the sign on a_n is negative ($a_n < 0$), and when n is even, the sign on a_n is positive ($a_n > 0$).

From this, we can suppose[2] that a general term for a_n is as follows:

$$a_n = (-1)^n (2n - 1)$$

Answer: $a_n = (-1)^n (2n - 1)$

Supplemental explanation:

For $n = 1, 2, 3, \ldots$, the value of $(-1)^n$ is as follows:

n	1	2	3	4	5	6	7	8	9	$\ldots$
$(-1)^n$	-1	1	-1	1	-1	1	-1	1	-1	$\ldots$

As you can see, $(-1)^n$ is 1 when n is even, and -1 when n is odd. You will often use $(-1)^n$ when you want to create a mathematical statement whose sign depends on the parity of n (whether n is even or odd).

---

[2]See Chapter 1 of *Math Girls* for a discussion of why such a conjecture may be questionable.

Problem 5-3 (Mathematical induction)

Use mathematical induction to prove that

$$1 + 2 + 3 + \cdots + n = \frac{n(n+1)}{2}$$

for a given positive integer n.

Answer 5-3 (Mathematical induction)

Define the following equation as $P(n)$:

$$1 + 2 + 3 + \cdots + n = \frac{n(n+1)}{2}.$$

Step A

We have that $P(1)$ holds, because

$$1 = \frac{1(1+1)}{2}.$$

Step B

Suppose that $P(k)$ holds. Then we can demonstrate that $P(k+1)$ holds, as follows:

$$1 + 2 + 3 + \cdots + k + (k+1)$$

$$= \frac{k(k+1)}{2} + (k+1) \qquad \text{from the assumption that } P(k) \text{ holds}$$

$$= \frac{k(k+1) + 2(k+1)}{2} \qquad \text{move } (k+1) \text{ to the numerator}$$

$$= \frac{(k+1)(k+2)}{2} \qquad \text{factor out } (k+1)$$

Therefore,

$$1 + 2 + 3 + \cdots + k + (k+1) = \frac{(k+1)(k+2)}{2}$$

holds, which means that $P(k+1)$ holds.

We have therefore shown by mathematical induction that $P(n)$ holds for every positive integer n. $\square$

Problem 5-4 (Mathematical induction)

For the sequence $\langle F_n \rangle$ in Problem 5-1, use mathematical induction to prove that

$$F_1 + F_2 + F_3 + \cdots + F_n = F_{n+2} - 1$$

for a given positive integer n.

Answer 5-4 (Mathematical induction)

Define the following equation as $Q(n)$:

$$F_1 + F_2 + F_3 + \cdots + F_n = F_{n+2} - 1$$

Step A

We are given that $F_1 = 1, F_3 = 2$, so $Q(1)$ holds, as follows:

$$F_1 = F_3 - 1.$$

Step B

Suppose that $Q(k)$ holds. Then we can demonstrate that $Q(k+1)$ holds, as follows:

$$
\begin{aligned}
&F_1 + F_2 + F_3 + \cdots + F_k + F_{k+1} \\
&= F_{k+2} - 1 + F_{k+1} && \text{from the assumption that } Q(k) \text{ holds} \\
&= F_{k+2} + F_{k+1} - 1 && \text{change order of the sum} \\
&= F_{k+3} - 1 && \text{because } F_{k+3} = F_{k+2} + F_{k+1}
\end{aligned}
$$

In other words, the following holds:

$$F_1 + F_2 + F_3 + \cdots + F_k + F_{k+1} = F_{(k+1)+2} - 1.$$

This means that $Q(k+1)$ holds.

We have therefore shown by mathematical induction that $Q(n)$ holds for every positive integer n. □

More Problems

"You learn by doing, not by thinking about doing."

In this section are some additional, slightly different problems for those who want to think more about the topics discussed in the conversations in this book. The answers won't be given here, and there won't necessarily be only one correct solution.

I hope you'll take your time and enjoy these problems, either alone or with a friend you can discuss them with.

EXTRA CHAPTER 1 PROBLEMS

Extra credit 1-X1 (Representation as mathematical expressions)

Represent the following mathematical objects as mathematical expressions:

- A positive integer leaving remainder 1 when divided by 2.

- A positive integer having 100 digits.

- An integer that's divisible by 2, 3, and 5.

Extra credit 1-X2 (Calculating remainders)

Suppose A and B are integers greater than or equal to 0.

Let a be the remainder after dividing A by 3, and let b be the remainder after dividing B by 3. What will be the remainder after dividing $A + B$ by 3?

Extra credit 1-X3 (A number with n digits)

In Chapter 1, the narrator gave a proof for a method of determining if a natural number less than 100 is a multiple of 3. He wanted to generalize this to any natural number, but was interrupted. Try giving a proof for the more general case in his place.

Here's a hint: try representing a natural number with n digits as

$$10^{n-1}a_{n-1} + \cdots + 10^2 a_2 + 10^1 a_1 + 10^0 a_0,$$

then factoring out a 3.

Extra credit 1-X4 (Determining factors in base-n)

At the end of Chapter 1, the narrator was thinking about methods of determining factors in base-n (see p. 24). Try giving that some thought yourself.

- When can you use the sum of a number's digits, as in the case of multiples of (decimal) 3 and 9?

- When can you use just the ones digit, as in the case of multiples of (decimal) 2 and 5?

Extra credit 1-X5 (Determining multiples of 1)

In Chapter 1, Yuri and the narrator discovered that the method for determining multiples of 3 and 9 are similar because both evenly divide 9. But note that 1 also evenly divides 9. So can the method for determining multiples of 3 and 9 be extended to 1?

EXTRA CHAPTER 2 PROBLEMS

Extra credit 2-X1 (Ulam's spiral)

Create your own Ulam's spirals. If you start from a different number, what happens to the pattern?

Extra credit 2-X2 (Primes and composites)

Prove that if a natural number n is a composite number, then $2^n - 1$ must be a composite number too.

(As an aside, numbers in the form $2^n - 1$ are called Mersenne numbers, and primes of that form are called Mersenne primes.)

Extra credit 2-X3 (The binomial $n^2 + n + 41$)

Prove that for a given natural number n, the value of the binomial $P(n) = n^2 + n + 41$ is not divisible by 2, 3, 5, or 7.

EXTRA CHAPTER 3 PROBLEMS

Extra credit 3-X1 (Discovering patterns)

In the table on p. 98, circle the binary numbers that have exactly two consecutive 1s (numbers like 01100 and 00110). Can you find any other common characteristics between such numbers? What about numbers that have exactly three consecutive 1s?

Extra credit 3-X2 (Discovering patterns)

In the table on p. 98, use lines to connect pairs of binary numbers that have opposite digits (pairs like 01100 and 10011). Do you see a pattern?

How about for pairs of numbers that reverse each other (pairs like 10100 and 00101)?

Extra credit 3-X3 (Binary numbers)

An n-digit binary number can represent decimal numbers 0 through $2^n - 1$. Think of a *really* big number, like one quadrillion (1,000,000,000,000,000), and figure out how many binary digits you would need to represent it.

EXTRA CHAPTER 4 PROBLEMS

Extra credit 4-X1 (Calculating backwards)

In the clock puzzles, a pattern was given and the narrator and Yuri searched for the number of times the count button had to be pressed to generate it. Try tackling this problem in reverse, and find a method for finding the resulting pattern after a given number of button presses.

Extra credit 4-X2 (Adding a clock)

Find a way to solve the clock puzzle after adding one more dial.

Extra credit 4-X3 (A new clock puzzle)

Try making a clock puzzle that has an n-clock, an $(n+1)$-clock, and an $(n+2)$-clock.

Extra credit 4-X4 (Breaking a code)

You're trying to break a code that uses pairs of upper- and lower-case Greek letters. The combinations used are listed in the tables below.

Upper	A B Γ Δ E Z H Θ I K
Lower	α β γ δ ε ζ η θ ι κ λ μ

Upper	Lower	Pair	Upper	Lower	Pair	Upper	Lower	Pair
A	α	Aα	A	ι	Aι	A	ε	Aε
B	β	Bβ	B	κ	Bκ	B	ζ	Bζ
Γ	γ	Γγ	Γ	λ	Γλ	Γ	η	Γη
Δ	δ	Δδ	Δ	μ	Δμ	Δ	θ	Δθ
E	ε	Eε	E	α	Eα	E	ι	Eι
Z	ζ	Zζ	Z	β	Zβ	Z	κ	Zκ
H	η	Hη	H	γ	Hγ	H	λ	Hλ
Θ	θ	Θθ	Θ	δ	Θδ	Θ	μ	Θμ
I	ι	Iι	I	ε	Iε	I	α	Iα
K	κ	Kκ	K	ζ	Kζ	K	β	Kβ
Λ	λ	Λλ	Λ	η	Λη	Λ	γ	Λγ
B	μ	Bμ	B	θ	Bθ	B	δ	Bδ
Γ	α	Γα	Γ	ι	Γι	Γ	ε	Γε
Δ	β	Δβ	Δ	κ	Δκ	Δ	ζ	Δζ
E	γ	Eγ	E	λ	Eλ	E	η	Eη
Z	δ	Zδ	Z	μ	Zμ	Z	θ	Zθ
H	ε	Hε	H	α	Hα	H	ι	Hι
Θ	ζ	Θζ	Θ	β	Θβ	Θ	κ	Θκ
I	η	Iη	I	γ	Iγ	I	λ	Iλ
K	θ	Kθ	K	δ	Kδ	K	μ	Kμ

You notice that some letter combinations appear in the code, while others do not. For example Aα is used, but Aβ is not.

Discover a rule that determines whether a given combination of upper- and lower-case letters will appear in the code.

Extra credit 4-X5 (Least common multiples)

The least common multiple of natural numbers a, b, and c is the smallest number that is evenly divisible by those numbers.

On p. 118, when Yuri asks, "Why'd we get [the least common multiple] this time?" the narrator responds, "Because 2, 3, and 5 are all primes." It's true that multiplying primes will give you their least common multiple, but the numbers don't have to be primes for that to work. For example, the least common multiple of $3, 4, 5$ is

$$3 \times 4 \times 5 = 60,$$

but 4 isn't a prime.

Under what conditions can you just multiply numbers together to get their least common multiple?

EXTRA CHAPTER 5 PROBLEMS

Extra credit 5-X1 (Mathematical induction)

Use mathematical induction to show that

$$1^3 + 2^3 + 3^3 + \cdots + n^3 = (1 + 2 + 3 + \cdots + n)^2$$

for a given natural number n (i.e., $n = 1, 2, 3, \ldots$).

Extra credit 5-X2 (Mathematical induction)

Find the error in the following proof:

Theorem
All people are the same age.

Proof
Let $Y(n)$ be the statement that all members of a group of n persons are the same age.

Step A
All members of a group of 1 person have the same age, because there is only one person in that group. $Y(1)$ thus holds.

Step B
Let us suppose that $Y(k)$ holds, and show that in that case $Y(k + 1)$ must also hold.

Arrange the $k + 1$ members of the group in a line, as shown in the diagram.

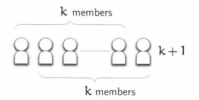

We are supposing that $Y(k)$ holds, so everyone in the group of k persons formed from excluding the rightmost person is the same age. Similarly, everyone in the group of k persons formed from excluding the leftmost person is the same age. From this, we can see that everyone in the group of $k + 1$ persons is the same age. Therefore, $Y(k + 1)$ holds.

We have thus shown by mathematical induction that $Y(n)$ holds for a given positive integer n. □

Extra credit 5-X3 (Mathematical induction)

What do you think of the following "proof"?

Theorem
A person having n dollars is not rich, for any positive integer value of n.

Proof
We prove the theorem using mathematical induction.

Step A
A person having \$1 is not rich.

Step B
If a person having \$$k$ is not rich, then neither is someone having \$$(k + 1)$, because \$1 cannot be the difference between wealth and poverty.

It thereby follows by mathematical induction that a person having n dollars is not rich, for a given positive integer value of n.   □

Hint: Approach this proof from two directions: If it is incorrect, what exactly is wrong with it? If you think it is correct, what does that imply?

Credit: Problem 5-X2 was adapted from a problem in *Concrete Mathematics*, by Graham, Knuth, and Patashnik (Addison-Wesley Professional, 1994).

Afterword

Thank you for reading this book. I hope you enjoyed it.

This book is a rearrangement of ten mathematical conversations I posted on the website *Cakes* as a serial feature called "Math Girls: Secret Notebooks." This is a series of fun conversations about fundamental mathematical concepts between four fictional characters: a junior high school student named Yuri, and three high school students, Tetra, Miruka, and the narrator. These are the main characters from *Math Girls*, a separate series of "mathematical romance" novels in which they tackle challenging topics from many areas of mathematics. I hope that once you're comfortable with the content in this series, you'll take on *Math Girls* as well.

As with the *Math Girls* series, this book was produced using LaTeX 2_ε and the AMS Euler font. I would like to thank Haruhiko Okumura for his book *Introduction to Creating Beautiful Documents with* LaTeX 2_ε, which was an invaluable aid during layout. I created the diagrams using OmniGraffle by The Omni Group.

I would also like to thank the following persons for proofreading my drafts and giving me invaluable feedback, as well as those who did so anonymously. Of course, any errors remaining in the book are solely the responsibility of the author.

Yuta Asami, Yusuke Ajiki, Tatsuya Igarashi, Tetsuya Ishiu, Ryuta Ishimoto, Kazuhiro Inaba, Ryuhei Uehara, Yoshiyuki Okutani, Midori Kawakami, Toshiya Kawashima, Iwao Kimura, Yuki Kutsuna, Jun Kudo, Kazuhiro Kezuka, Kayo Kotaki, Akiko Sakaguchi, Tomofumi Takata, Hiroaki Hanada, Aya Hayashi, Hiroshi Fujita, Yutori Bonten (Medaka College), Masahide Maehara, Nami Masuda, Kiyoshi Miyake, Ken Murai, Yusuke Muraoka, Kenta Murata (mrkn), Takeshi Yamaguchi

I would like to thank my editor at Softbank Creative, Kimio Nozawa, for his continuous support throughout both the *Math Girls* and *Math Girls Talk About...* series.

I thank Sadaaki Kato, of Cakes.

I thank all my readers, for the support they've given my writing.

I thank my dearest wife and our two sons.

And I thank you, for having read this far. I hope to see you again in the next book in this series.

Hiroshi Yuki

December, 2013

http://www.hyuki.com/girl/

Index

Other works by Hiroshi Yuki

(in English)

- *Math Girls*, Bento Books, 2011

- *Math Girls 2: Fermat's Last Theorem*, Bento Books, 2012

- *Math Girls Manga*, Bento Books, 2013

- *Math Girls Talk About Equations & Graphs*, Bento Books, 2014

(in Japanese)

- *The Essence of C Programming*, Softbank, 1993 (revised 1996)

- *C Programming Lessons, Introduction*, Softbank, 1994 (Second edition, 1998)

- *C Programming Lessons, Grammar*, Softbank, 1995

- *An Introduction to CGI with Perl, Basics*, Softbank Publishing, 1998

- *An Introduction to CGI with Perl, Applications*, Softbank Publishing, 1998

- *Java Programming Lessons (Vols. I & II)*, Softbank Publishing, 1999 (revised 2003)

- *Perl Programming Lessons, Basics*, Softbank Publishing, 2001

- *Learning Design Patterns with Java*, Softbank Publishing, 2001 (revised and expanded, 2004)

- *Learning Design Patterns with Java, Multithreading Edition*, Softbank Publishing, 2002

- *Hiroshi Yuki's Perl Quizzes*, Softbank Publishing, 2002

- *Introduction to Cryptography Technology*, Softbank Publishing, 2003

- *Hiroshi Yuki's Introduction to Wikis*, Impress, 2004

- *Math for Programmers*, Softbank Publishing, 2005

- *Java Programming Lessons, Revised and Expanded (Vols. I & II)*, Softbank Creative, 2005

- *Learning Design Patterns with Java, Multithreading Edition, Revised Second Edition*, Softbank Creative, 2006

- *Revised C Programming Lessons, Introduction*, Softbank Creative, 2006

- *Revised C Programming Lessons, Grammar*, Softbank Creative, 2006

- *Revised Perl Programming Lessons, Basics*, Softbank Creative, 2006

- *Introduction to Refactoring with Java*, Softbank Creative, 2007

- *Math Girls / Fermat's Last Theorem*, Softbank Creative, 2008

- *Revised Introduction to Cryptography Technology*, Softbank Creative, 2008

- *Math Girls Comic (Vols. I & II)*, Media Factory, 2009

- *Math Girls / Gödel's Incompleteness Theorems*, Softbank Creative, 2009

- *Math Girls / Randomized Algorithms*, Softbank Creative, 2011

- *Math Girls / Galois Theory*, Softbank Creative, 2012

- *Java Programming Lessons, Third Edition (Vols. I & II)*, Softbank Creative, 2012

- *Etiquette in Writing Mathematical Statements: Fundamentals*, Chikuma Shobo, 2013

- *Math Girls Secret Notebook / Equations & Graphs*, Softbank Creative, 2013

- *Math Girls Secret Notebook / Let's Play with the Integers*, Softbank Creative, 2013

- *The Birth of Math Girls,* Softbank Creative, 2013

- *Math Girls Secret Notebook / Round Trigonometric Functions*, Softbank Creative, 2014

58306427R00143

Made in the USA
Columbia, SC
19 May 2019